Praise for THRILLE

"Dr. Hart is one of the wisest men on the planet. I have worked with people and had friends who could not live without the rush of a recent thrill. Now I have a great resource for them."

—Stephen Arterburn
Author, *Healing Is a Choice*

"We live in a world gone completely high-tech with little or no time to stop and enjoy the simple pleasures God created: a stunning sunrise or sunset or a fragrant rose, the simple joys of life. Dr. Archibald Hart not only offers scientifically proven research to explain the growing phenomenon of a life without joy but also outlines the steps toward recovering the pleasures in life that God created. Every one of us needs to read this book."

—Robert Anthony Schuller
Senior Pastor, The Crystal Cathedral and *The Hour of Power*

"An excellent resource for counselors and for those who want to slow down, get control, and embrace the finer things of life. Arch teaches how to live joyfully."

—Dr. Tim Clinton
President, American Association of Christian Counselors, and Author, *Turn Your Life Around*

"Arch Hart's ability to keep our leadership focus boldly realistic, clear-headed, and genuinely holy is well established. This newest book is our summons to meet again in his classroom—to grow in wisdom and increase in true effectiveness."

—Jack W. Hayford
President, International Foursquare Churches,
Chancellor, The King's College and Seminary,
and Founding Pastor, The Church On The Way

THRILLED TO
DEATH

Published in Nashville, TN, by Thomas Nelson. Thomas Nelson is a trademark of Thomas Nelson, Inc.

Library of Congress Cataloging-in-Publication Data
Hart, Archibald D.
  Thrilled to death : how the endless pursuit of pleasure is leaving us numb / Archibald Hart.
      p. cm.
  Includes bibliographical references.
  ISBN 10: 0-8499-1852-9
  ISBN 13: 978-0-8499-1852-0 (pbk.)
  1. Pleasure. I. Title.
BF515.H37 2007
152.4'2--dc22
                                                                      2007013507

Printed in the United States of America
07 08 09 10 11 RRD 5 4 3 2 1

THRILLED TO
DEATH

[how the endless pursuit *of* pleasure is leaving us numb]

Dr. Archibald D. Hart

THOMAS NELSON
Since 1798

NASHVILLE   DALLAS   MEXICO CITY   RIO DE JANEIRO   BEIJING

[contents]

[acknowledgments]

As every author knows, the hardest part of any book to write is the acknowledgments page. Not because one doesn't know who to thank, but every book is the product of so many influences that it is impossible to do justice and acknowledge all who have played an important part in shaping a book. This book is no exception.

While there are a few who must be mentioned, I particularly want to express my appreciation to the many whose names must remain private but to whom I am nevertheless deeply indebted for the influence they have had over my life. Top of this list are the many patients I have had over the years. I often wonder whether psychotherapy benefits the patient more than the psychotherapist or the other way around. Maybe I've just been fortunate because in my case, I have been the primary beneficiary of the many intimate therapy hours spent with them. I am in their debt more than they realize. (Let me hasten to add that while the stories in this book are generally true, they reflect an amalgam of many, not any one particular patient. All identifying information has been concealed and confidentiality protected.)

Now to those whose help is especially appreciated, I want to thank the staff of Thomas Nelson, starting with Ernie Owen, who published my first book and has never given up on me as a writer, and David Moberg, a longtime supporter. To Debbie Wickwire, for her unfailing trust in the topic of this book and her expertise in guiding its form and content, I owe special gratitude. And to my editor, Jennifer Stair, who so expertly guided me through the maze of style sheets and crisp writing, I am particularly indebted.

Nearer home I am indebted to my oldest daughter, Dr. Catherine Hart Weber, for her help in several important areas, and to my dear wife, Kathleen, who patiently and lovingly read and reread drafts of each chapter, encouraging me to clarify and qualify whenever it was warranted. I couldn't imagine ever being able to write a book without her help.

To all of you I say, *Baie dankie*—that's Afrikaans for the deepest felt thankfulness one could possibly express.

[introduction]
WHY WE ARE BEING "THRILLED TO DEATH"

Pleasure. Everyone knows what it feels like: it is the delight of a mouthful of Sees candy, or the afterglow a young man feels after a date with the girl he has fallen in love with. For a businessman, it is clinching a sale; for a mother, it is her baby's first smile. For me, it is completing a building project around the house or finally getting all the bugs out of a computer program I am writing for my lab research. The pursuit of pleasure underlies almost everything we try to achieve in life.

Yet today we have taken the pursuit of pleasure too far, and in so doing we have lost the ability to experience the very pleasure we are pursuing. As this book will show, consistent overuse of the brain's pleasure circuits causes us to lose our capacity to experience pleasure. When we seek pleasure primarily through extreme, overstimulating thrills, we hijack our brain's pleasure system and rob ourselves of the ability to experience pleasure from simple things. Literally, we are being *thrilled to death*—to the *death* of our ability to experience genuine pleasure.

> We have taken the pursuit of pleasure too far, and in so doing we have lost the ability to experience the very pleasure we are pursuing.

The discoveries being made with new brain-imaging techniques help us better understand how the stress of modern life contributes to our emotional numbing. Whereas this loss of pleasure, called *anhedonia*, was previously linked only to serious emotional disorders like depression, schizophrenia, and drug addictions, we are now seeing it in otherwise healthy people. We are all, to some extent, losing our ability to gain pleasure from normally pleasurable experiences. This is the topic of this book.

Compared to the ease with which, say, our grandparents were able to find delight in relatively low-stimulating activities, it now takes an enormously high level of stimulation to deliver us just a modicum of enjoyment. There is a pervasive emotional numbness overtaking us. Just ask my grandchildren, and they will tell you exactly what it feels like. Many people now report what someone has called *a joyless existence*—a life where even the most significant accomplishments leave you feeling empty, and what used to bring great excitement and happiness now leaves you numb and unsatisfied.

> We are all, to some extent, losing our ability to gain pleasure from normally pleasurable experiences.

Anhedonia is no longer the exclusive domain of emotional disorders. It is becoming the experience of a lot of ordinary people like you and me. Increasingly, we are finding it difficult to extract ordinary enjoyment out of our chaotic world.

To my Christian readers, I would also like to add that modern worship styles and spiritual practices, when not balanced with contemplative or reflective practices, can also contribute to the hijacking of the brain's pleasure system.

This book will, I trust, help you come to terms with the sources of your own emotional numbing. In the first part of this book, I will explore the reasons for the loss of your pleasure and give some guidance on how you and your children can avoid the addiction pitfalls that accompany the emergence of anhedonia. Then in the second part of this book, I will present seven steps that can help you recover your pleasure system. Anhedonia is very much like an addiction, so the term *recover* is very appropriate. Each of the seven steps will have several specific exercises. I encourage you to first read through all of them and then go back to step one and work through the exercises.

Before you begin, let me give an overarching principle: a healthy pleasure system is best achieved if you spread your pleasure around. We should be able to derive pleasure from our work, but also from our play or recreation time; from our hobbies, but also from time spent with our family; from personal "me" time, but also from social activities; from private meditation, but also from corporate worship. As in so many things in life, it's all about balance. The pleasure you get from life is the accumulation of the pleasure you take from all aspects of your life.

> A healthy pleasure system is best achieved if you spread your pleasure around.

So join me as I show you how to recover your pleasure and enjoy enduring, authentic happiness.

—Archibald D. Hart, PhD

part
one

THE INABILITY *to* EXPERIENCE PLEASURE

WHERE HAS ALL OUR PLEASURE GONE?

I can think of nothing less pleasurable
than a life devoted to pleasure.
—JOHN D. ROCKEFELLER

From the information I gleaned in my first interview with him, Brian seemed like someone to be envied. He had it all! He grew up in the best of neighborhoods with caring parents who provided him with the best education. Then followed a great marriage and two adorable children. To be honest, I was tempted to envy Brian that Thursday morning during our first session. It was hard to believe that he needed help. He certainly didn't show any outward signs of distress.

But as the session proceeded and we pulled back the veil of privacy, it all came flooding out. For many of the reasons that I will be describing in this book, Brian was extremely unhappy. He had what most of us would consider a very successful life. At age thirty-four he had been promoted to division sales manager, complete with a company car and sizeable benefits package. He was active in his church and community, and his family was looking forward to their annual vacation in a few weeks. "So why do I feel so empty?" he asked me. "I have everything I could have ever hoped for, but I just can't seem to enjoy any of it. No matter what I achieve or acquire, it's like I'm totally numb inside. What's wrong with me?"

> Our continuous pursuit of high stimulation is snuffing out our ability to experience genuine pleasure in simple things.

A certain numbness had become his regular feeling. He had been a vibrant, outgoing, and energetic person, but now all he felt was persistent apathy. It was now hard for him to be enthusiastic about anything. He had lost interest in activities that used to excite him, and now only *wow* experiences grabbed him. And on top of all of this, he had lost his ability to extract even the slightest pleasure out of the ordinary things of life.

It's called *anhedonia*—a feeling of joylessness and cheerlessness. Everyone feels it to some extent these days, and it's not going to go away. In our fast-paced, pleasure-seeking society, we are obsessed with increasing our level of excitement to feel a sense of pleasure. When we go to the movies, we expect the action sequences to be more thrilling and spectacular than before. Our music must be louder and edgier than the last album. Even in our churches, preachers must out-wow their last sermon or we might not go back again. We have become addictively dependent on persistent thrills and kicks.

What's bad about this? The problem is that we are being thrilled to death! Our continuous pursuit of high stimulation is snuffing out our ability to experience genuine pleasure in simple things.

Scientists who are exploring anhedonia believe not only that we are slowly losing our capacity for pleasure, but that this condition might be a major factor in many emotional problems, such as depression and anxiety, as well as contributing to addictions to sex, work, drugs, and other addicting behaviors. More alarming to me is that anhedonia is impacting our children and teenagers to a greater extent than parents, and if we don't take action to correct it, I pity where the next generation is headed. Deriving pleasure from the ordinary and healthy experiences of life will be a thing of the past. We will come to rely entirely on psychotropic medications for our happiness—and this happiness will only be artificial at best.

WHAT IS ANHEDONIA?

Anhedonia refers to the reduced ability to experience pleasure. And it is a phenomenon that is growing in leaps and bounds. Scientists are adamant that as we push the stress level and exciting stimulation higher and higher, we are literally overloading the pathways to the pleasure center of the brain. This overload causes our brain's pleasure center to demand a further increase in the level of stimulation before delivering more feelings of pleasure. This results in a decline in our pleasure system's ability to deliver enjoyment out of ordinary, simple things. I see this process at work in my patients, friends and family, and even in myself.

> Anhedonia refers to the reduced ability to experience pleasure.

I must confess that I know about a diminished pleasure response all too well. Of course, I had seen patients who were anhedonic, but mostly we believed that only people with severe depression or a mental disorder could be so profoundly lacking in pleasure. But my experience of anhedonia felt different.

My life had always been full of pleasurable experiences. I have never lacked any ability to turn on my pleasure circuits. My hobbies, for instance, are a great source of enjoyment—even today. I can't begin to describe the hours of delight I have enjoyed in, for instance, crafting gold rings for my wife and my daughters. I make a habit of collecting *old* gold when I travel back to my country of birth, South Africa, one of the world's great gold producers. In fact, I grew up in a gold mining town so cannot but be obsessed with its beauty.

I can also derive immense satisfaction from completing a computer program I need for my research, or building a physiological instrument I need for my laboratory, or reroofing a part of my house, or repairing my car. I can plot and scheme and create so much pleasurable experiences that I sometimes worry about not living long enough to accomplish all the things I want to accomplish. And I am talking about things I *want* to do, not work I *have* to do There's a big difference. But every now and again without expecting it, I feel that I couldn't be bothered. Pleasure is gone. Nothing can make me feel pleasure. It's as if something in my brain switches off, and life feels boring, blah, blunted, and bland. (That little alliteration did give me a pleasure boost.)

> The lack of ability to experience pleasure affects every aspect of our lives.

And many of you reading this book feel the same. Up and down on the pleasure scale—like a yo-yo. Many today are beginning to suffer from an emotional disorder called *hedonic dysregulation*. In simple terms, it means that your brain's pleasure center is not working properly. When it should be giving you pleasure, it doesn't.

But if only our disregulated pleasure centers would confine themselves to the realm of pleasure, I would not bother to write this book. Anhedonia, in and of itself, is no big deal when you put it in life's larger perspective. But other consequences of anhedonia are much more serious and pervasive than this. The lack of ability to experience pleasure affects every aspect of our lives, from sexuality to addictions, from relationships to spirituality. Even our capacity to experience God to the fullest is seriously compromised when we suffer from even the mildest form of anhedonia.

Anhedonia is a disorder that is here to stay, and it already has its tentacles in many of us.

ANHEDONIA'S INNER WORLD

The inner world of severely anhedonic people can be summed up by the following comment of a high-achieving, success-driven patient: "My food seems tasteless. A beautiful woman no longer attracts me. Music no longer pleases me. I don't care if I never go to a movie again. My friends seem dull. I look forward to nothing. I don't want to die, but I don't care about living. I don't get a kick out of anything, except perhaps making some big deal come to reality."

And these are not the sentiments of a severely depressed patient. They are the experience of a lot of ordinary people. I know, because I meet them every day, wherever I go. I've just returned from a three-country speaking tour and found anhedonic people in South Africa, Germany, and Switzerland, just as I have in the United States.

How does anhedonia show itself? Anhedonic people smile very weakly, if at all. Someone cracks a joke, but they don't laugh when everyone else is laughing. They express little or no feelings even when grief or mourning is the appropriate emotion. The more severe the anhedonia, the more completely it shuts down the pleasure system and experience of any joyful feelings. Eventually it can cause a severe emotional disorder such as major depression. For most of us who suffer from what is called *stress-induced anhedonia*, however, the loss of pleasure sensitivity is more insidious and less severe, though still problematic. There's no fun to be had when you go through life always seeking that *wow* experience to scrape together a little bit of pleasure.

If you are wondering just how lacking you are in your ability to extract real pleasure from life, be patient. I will offer a test for anhedonia in the next chapter. This test will help you get a clearer picture of just how far down the road to annihilation you have taken your pleasure system.

I can best clarify what anhedonia feels like through two short stories.

Suzie has just given birth to her first child. It wasn't a very difficult labor, and everything went like clockwork. She had looked forward with great anticipation to having a baby, especially since she miscarried her first baby—a devastating loss. This baby would make up for her pain and fear that she would never be able to have a second chance at motherhood. So you can imagine her dismay when in the moments after the nurse placed her newborn baby in her arms, she felt no joy. *It must be the effect of the drugs, or maybe I am just exhausted,* she thought. *Tomorrow I will feel more excited.* But she didn't. Holding her baby, flesh of her flesh, left her feeling numb. No joy or pleasure whatsoever as she coddled this helpless, dependent gift of life. Welcome to anhedonia! In this case, it is being caused by postpartum depression.

Mary is a teenager. She's been learning to drive and was planning on getting a job soon so she could pay the matching half her father had promised and buy her own car. Most of her friends already had wheels, and this token of emerging adulthood meant a lot to her. She took her driving test and aced it. Walking back to the car with her license in hand, her father asked her how she felt. "Nothing," was her reply. He wasn't very surprised, since this has been her tone for some time now. Despite eagerly anticipating this significant milestone in her life, she was totally unmoved. Teenage anhedonia.

EVERYONE NEEDS TO KNOW ABOUT ANHEDONIA

The term *anhedonia* is derived from the Greek *a-* (without), and *hedone* (pleasure, delight). The word *hedone* is also the root of *hedonism* (a philosophy that emphasizes pleasure as an aim of life, and often considered to be sinful in Christian circles), *hedonist* (a pleasure seeker), and *hedonophobia* (an excessive fear of feeling pleasure).

To use metaphoric language, anhedonia is not having anything in your life that can move your heart. Your happiness is deadened because your joy is missing.

To the mental health professionals reading this book, let me say that I am not using the term *anhedonia* in the strict clinical sense. As every psychologist and psychiatrist knows, severe anhedonia is the cardinal symptom of such disorders as major depression and schizophrenia. No, I am talking about a more subtle and insidious loss, a decline over time of the ability to find joy in small events and simple experiences while being pushed into ever increasing levels of stimulation. What used to make us feel ecstatic now has no power to thrill us.

> Anhedonia is not having anything in your life that can move your heart.

It is the decline of the pleasure we were born with and nature intended us to enjoy before the modern, excessive pursuit of excitement took over and hijacked the brain's pleasure system. In a real sense, we have lost our pleasure by becoming addicted to pleasure that is outside the box of normal existence.

Pastors also know very well what I mean here. I do a lot of seminars for clergy. When they are young, just starting out on their calling and fresh from seminary, they could take great joy in what they were able to do for God. Every day was a thrilling adventure. But with time, subject to many of the factors I will be sharing in this book, something changed. Pleasure was lost. As one pastor said to me recently, "I no longer feel any pleasure in my work as a pastor. I don't enjoy my wife and family. And the other night, it dawned on me that I don't even find any pleasure in God anymore." An honest comment—but indicative of how widespread anhedonia has become.

But take heart, this is not a pessimistic book. You can repair the part of your brain that delivers deep, satisfying pleasure and become a joyful, happy person again. I know. I did it for myself. And I've helped many others do it as well.

UNCOVERING THE BRAIN'S PLEASURE SYSTEM

Simply put, anhedonia, the reduced ability to experience pleasure, is brought on, paradoxically, by the excessive pursuit of pleasure. Mainly it develops out of the high amount of stress most of us experience today. It is a by-product of the fantastic technological improvements in our world. We now have such a high level of stimulation that we can escape boredom in an instant.

> You can repair the part of your brain that delivers deep, satisfying pleasure and become a joyful, happy person again.

Just think about it. Are you ever lonely? Just log on to your favorite Internet chat group and bye-bye loneliness. Bored? Turn on your iPod or watch a movie on your portable DVD player. Fed up? Grab your cell phone and text-message the person you are ticked off with to get it off your chest. Of course, your stress level will go higher when twenty seconds later you get a message back, venting on you. Need to work on a project or homework? Put your iPod earpiece in one ear, your cell phone earpiece in the other, turn on your laptop to check your e-mail, and now you can concentrate on your project or homework.

All of this stimulates your brain to the point of overload. Technology is revolutionizing our lives but ravaging our brains. A reasonable use of technology is good, but too much is bad as we will see.

THE BRAIN'S PLEASURE CENTER

This brings me to the central focus of this book. The problem of anhedonia revolves around an important part of the brain that is increasingly getting the attention of scientists. To really grasp the problem of anhedonia, you have to understand a little about how the brain works to deliver us pleasure. So bear with me.

Not too many years ago, scientists discovered that the brains of both humans and animals had what they called a *reward* or *pleasure* center. This hardwired system in the brain is responsible for creating the feeling we call pleasure. There are several pathways to this center, depending on what is creating the pleasure. This specific part of the brain has one exclusive and exquisite purpose: to deliver pleasure to our consciousness. This remarkable discovery happened quite by accident, and it's a story worth telling here.

In 1954 two researchers, Olds and Milner, were experimenting with implanted electrodes in a rat. They discovered that when they sent a small electric signal in one particular location in the brain, the animal would go into an unaccountable rage. They had discovered that the brain had a *rage* center. Each time this center was electrically stimulated, the animal would go into a rage and then stop as soon as the signal stopped.

One day, quite by mistake, the researchers put the electrode into an adjacent area. When they applied the signal, instead of creating a rage response, the animal seemed to like it. Really like it! So they set up a lever that the rat could press and deliver electrical signals to this newly discovered part of the brain whenever it chose to. And it chose to, all right. Again and again.

This area in the brain—which exists in all animals, including humans—was named the *locus accumbens*, but it is more commonly called the pleasure center. Very much later it was discovered that there are several centers in the brain that work together to deliver pleasure, but for the purpose in this book I will simply refer to the complex connections that help us know when something is pleasurable as the *pleasure system*. At the heart of this pleasure system is the pleasure center.

To show just how powerful this pleasure center is, controlled animal experiments with rats that could self-administer shots of pleasure as often as desired found that they would continue to do so as often as possible. One rat achieved a rate of ten thousand presses on the lever an hour. An animal could self-stimulate all day and night without rest and would forgo food and sex and even cross a painful grid that gave severe shocks to the feet to get to that pleasure-delivering lever.

The potency of this electrical stimulation is most dramatically illustrated in a classic experiment where the rats suffered self-imposed starvation when forced to make a choice between obtaining food and water or electrical brain stimulation. They chose pleasure to the point of dying.

THERE IS NEVER ENOUGH PLEASURE
TO SATISFY THE BRAIN

The researchers went even further in their experiments and found that not only is the pleasure system of the brain the superpotent deliverer of euphoric joy, but when it is stimulated directly, as when electrical signals are sent through implanted electrodes directly to the pleasure center, the animal is never fully satisfied. It's the same with humans. There is no limit to the craving for pleasure. This pleasure is a barrel without a bottom—it never gets full. The more you give it, the more it wants.

> This pleasure is a barrel without a bottom—it never gets full. The more you give it, the more it wants.

We need to keep this fact in mind as we proceed to explore the many ways we can inadvertently wipe out our ability to derive joy from our pleasure center. It is a system that does not know when enough is enough. It takes a higher system to control it and tell it to quit demanding more and more. In a healthy brain, for instance, eating good food eventually reaches satiation, and we stop eating—hopefully. But an anhedonic brain is never fully satisfied and thus will continue to eat, contributing to obesity and food addictions.

CAUSES OF ANHEDONIA—RATS ON A WHEEL

According to several researchers, modern humans have to keep running after things that make us feel better—success, achievements, addictions, and all that we can consume. This process is accurately called the *hedonic treadmill* by those scientists who study happiness.

Why, only yesterday I took my adorable puppy to the pet store to buy food for him. Let me introduce him. His name is Andy, which stands for *And-he-brought-joy*. He's a mongrel, a mix between a dachshund and a chihuahua, with soulful brown eyes. A more loving creature on God's earth you will never find.

On this occasion we walked into the pet store, and I noticed some small cages across the aisle with rat wheels in them, spinning like crazy. Andy eagerly pulled at his leash, wanting to take a closer look, so we walked over to the cages. I was amused by the diminutive rats running inside the tiny wheels as if their lives depended on it.

As I stood watching, I thought about the popular analogy between rats running in their wheels and the way many of us live. In some ways, we are all like rats on a wheel—running like mad but not really going anywhere. The more possessions we acquire, the more we want, so we turn the wheel again. The more success we achieve, the more we strive to repeat it, so round and round we go.

Is this a problem? Yes it is, according to many scientists. Keeping our wheels turning leaves no time to enjoy the journey. More notably, we have to keep boosting our level of pleasure as we go. Each turn of the wheel demands another turn. If we let up, anhedonia will take over.

> In some ways, we are all like rats on a wheel—running like mad but not really going anywhere.

I have yet to meet any extremely successful people who can honestly say they are happier now than when they started their quest for greatness without making some special effort to remain happy. If you can honestly say that extreme success by itself and without any other help has brought total and abiding happiness to you, then I want to hear from you. You deserve to be put on display in the Smithsonian.

So where does abiding, authentic happiness come from? We'll come to that later in the book. Before I can offer an answer to this question, you need to have a better understanding of the brain's pleasure system, how it works, and what undermines it.

ANHEDONIA ON THE MARCH

Now I come to the bad news. But don't despair. I promise it will get better as you read. Pleasure is a healthy and necessary part of human experience. It is what enables us to experience a beautiful life. But when we lose our ability to experience pleasure, we are in a lot of trouble. It can cause some of the most pathological of conditions and rob you of happiness. And it is becoming increasingly common.

Many prominent people have suffered from profound anhedonia. I don't want to take too much space here in discussing them, but one example will suffice to describe this problem. I came across this report of one prominent person who suffered anhedonia: "Terry Bradshaw, the Hall of Fame quarterback, made a startling disclosure in 2003: 'I didn't understand that after every Super Bowl victory, I could find no pleasure in what I'd done.'"[1]

> Pleasure is a healthy and necessary part of human experience. It is what enables us to experience a beautiful life.

Now isn't this alarming? Wouldn't you feel elated after leading your team to a Super Bowl victory? I would think so. But Bradshaw's admission that he was unable to experience any pleasure is consistent with what anhedonia does. And more and more people are beginning to experience it.

Some researchers have suggested that anhedonia is becoming epidemic, and I believe this also. Sometimes anhedonia accompanies depression, but increasingly we are seeing it in nondepressed people. I see it in myself. I see it in members of my family. And I see it more than ever before in my patients and the pastors I encounter in my seminars. It's not going to go away—if anything, anhedonia is becoming increasingly prevalent.

DISCOVERING THE BRAIN'S PLEASURE CENTER

Before we can examine in more detail the problem of anhedonia, we need to understand how the brain experiences pleasure. So please bear with me while I give you a brief description. It will help you better understand how you can prevent and recover from this now pervasive problem.

While, for the sake of simplicity, I talk about the pleasure center as if it is just a single part of the brain, it actually takes several brain centers to deliver the feeling of pleasure. At least three regions are connected by what is called the pleasure or reward *bundle*. In a system that is quite awesome, this part of the brain is activated by anything that gives pleasure, and this pleasure is then rewarded in such a way that it leads to repetition of the gratifying action. It's as if the brain wants you to be joyful and, therefore, helps to strengthen your ability to repeat the joyful experience.

Figure 1 is a simplified diagram showing how different pathways carry signals to the brain's pleasure center. As you will see, the process for getting pleasure is the same for simple, fun activities as it is for cocaine or other addictions. We only have one pleasure center, and all pleasures have to pass through this center. If these pathways are blocked, we become anhedonic and cannot experience pleasure.

PATHWAYS TO THE PLEASURE CENTER

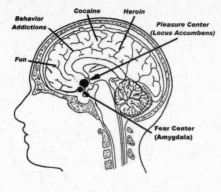

FIGURE 1

A FAMOUS EXPERIMENT

The discovery of how the brain delivers pleasure in humans is rather re-markable. It all started in the 1960s when an outlandish and ethically questionable experiment was conducted by a psychiatrist at Tulane University in New Orleans. He had a patient who suffered from depression, schizophrenia, intractable pain, and suicidal symptoms, so since no effective treatment was available, the psychiatrist decided to drown out all his illnesses with an overload of pleasure. After all, these disorders all had one thing in common: the patient was incapable of experiencing any pleasure—he was anhedonic.

An electrode was implanted deep within the pleasure center of the patient's brain. As we have already discussed in this book, whenever the center of rats was stimulated with mild shocks, the animals became euphoric. So the psychiatrist wanted to see if his patient could be made to feel euphoria the same way and thus be cured of his ailments.

The patient reported that he did feel better. Unfortunately, the good feelings didn't last. As soon as the stimulating current was turned off, the pleasurable feelings went away. And when the patient was given the control switch so that he could press it at will, he kept pressing it—again and again, thousands of times. That psychiatrist then went on to do other research, and the discovery of a pleasure center in the brain lay dormant for several decades.

In the early 1980s, another more alarming discovery was made. The pleasure center not only gives joy, but it also acts as a reward center by rewarding behaviors that bring joy. The chemical that sends the messages rushing around the brain to this reward system was found to be the neurotransmitter, dopamine. That's the good news. The bad news is that this system can so powerfully reward pleasurable experiences that it can also set up a pervasive dependence on these pleasures when abused, leading to forms of addiction.

> Too much of a good thing, including pleasure, is bad for our brain.

In the years that followed, all addictions became linked to this system. Sex, drugs, gambling, food—in every addictive behavior imaginable, this brain area is implicated. Thousands of studies, millions of dollars in research, and entire scientific careers have revolved around understanding this tiny little part of the brain. Since its role is to make us feel good, it's been called the brain's *G spot*. When we pursue the right pleasures and nurture this part of the brain, we can experience all the delights—physical, emotional, and spiritual—that are imaginable. But if we abuse this system, we lose the ability to fully enjoy any of these delights.

The ability to experience pleasure is a very good thing—in fact, it's essential to a good life. Yet too much of a good thing, including pleasure, is bad for our brain. It hijacks the pleasure center, making it possible for only very exciting things, like drugs or sex, to deliver pleasure. Scientists are clear in stating that there is a natural limit to pleasure, and when we overstep this limit, pleasure is lost. By definition, pleasure cannot be long lasting. Like all systems in the body, the brain's pleasure system needs time for rest and recovery. In the chapters to come, we will see how much that is happening in our modern world is a time bomb for widespread anhedonia.

HOW PLEASURE IS LOST

To illustrate the process by which the pleasure center can be hijacked, I have prepared three simple diagrams. These show the progression from a healthy pleasure system that can help you enjoy the pleasures to be derived from ordinary life events, to the state of anhedonia, where the barrier to the pleasure center prevents all signals from getting there.

Figure 2 shows a normal pathway to the pleasure center. Signals flow freely along the dopamine pathways and stimulate our pleasure center. Even the simple things of life are pleasurable. But as Figure 3 shows, when we overstimulate our pleasure system, the flooding of dopamine begins to set up a barrier, and now it takes an ever-increasing stimulating pleasure to get over the barrier. This is called the *addictive process* because, as with all addictions, you have to keep upping the ante on the stimulation, or you lose the feeling of pleasure.

Finally, as shown in Figure 4, full-blown anhedonia develops when

> Severe anhedonia . . . is now increasingly becoming the experience of ordinary people like you and me.

THE ANHEDONIA PROCESS

At the start, enjoyment has free access to the pleasure center

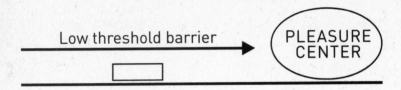

Figure 2: A Healthy Pleasure Response

Overstimulation starts to raise the barrier to the pleasure center due to dopamine **flooding**

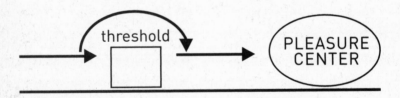

Figure 3: Starting to Block the Pleasure Center

the dopamine flooding is so severe and the barrier so high that only major pleasures, such as those found in many drugs or addicting behaviors (sexual, gambling, thrill seeking), can deliver any pleasure to our brain. Severe anhedonia used to be seen only in disorders such as major depression, but it is now increasingly becoming the experience of ordinary people like you and me.

THE ANHEDONIA PROCESS
Full-blown Anhedonia

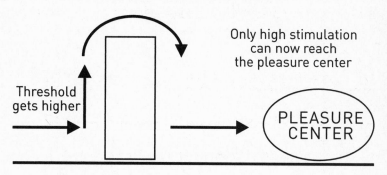

Figure 4: Fully Developed, Severe Anhedonia

Is there a solution? Can we protect ourselves from such pleasure robbing experiences? Yes we can. And that is what this book is all about.

THE MANY PATHWAYS
TO PLEASURE

To do something, say something, see something,
before anybody else—
these are things that confer a pleasure
compared with which other pleasures are tame.
—MARK TWAIN

As I write this chapter, I am in a condo on the beach in Waikiki overlooking the ocean. I've just come from a conference at which my wife and I spoke on the topic of this book. During my presentation, I asked the large audience to reflect for a moment on this question: Do you feel the same level of pleasure in your life now as you did as a child?

I asked those present to raise their hands if they did. Not one hand in the room was raised. I think I would have received the same nonresponse from any group I was addressing. Childhood thrills are often left behind in childhood. Somewhere along the way, these pleasures simply died as we overstimulated our pleasure systems to the point of becoming thrilled to death.

Obviously, as one gets older, some anhedonia is bound to develop. Life loses its novelty. Emotional pain inevitably intrudes and robs us of some of our joy. As a child, I remember how enthralled I was with butterflies. Their beautiful patterns were spellbinding to my young eyes. At five, I saved up my pocket money and bought a magnifying glass so I could examine their wings. I even tried to build a microscope out of a couple of glass bottles. But now, although I still think butterfly wings are pretty, my fascination with and pleasure derived from them have faded.

> Our overindulgence in seeking too much stimulation for our brain's pleasure center is slowly disregulating it, causing it to lose its power to enthrall.

True, as you get older, you get used to pretty things, so it is inevitable that they will lose some of their awesomeness. But what is happening to our pleasure system is more serious than this. I am convinced that we have turned a corner on pleasure and that our overindulgence in seeking too much stimulation for our brain's pleasure center is slowly disregulating it, causing it to lose its power to enthrall.

I am convinced that a lot of this *pleasure loss* is the result of our overstress and overdependence on high stimulation.

MANY ROADS TO PLEASURE

As I mentioned in the first chapter, there are many doorways to the brain's pleasure system. And each doorway has several pathways. It's very much like going to Disneyland. You go through the main gate and are faced with several options—Pirates of the Caribbean? Mad Tea Party? Tarzan's Treehouse or Space Mountain? So many pathways to pleasure.

The problem with having so many paths to pleasure is that we don't know whether a particular pleasure we are pursuing is good for us or bad, healthy or unhealthy. They all feel good in their own ways. Despite having more sources of pleasure than ever before in history, we are probably the unhappiest people who have ever lived. To some extent, all of us are now suffering from some degree of anhedonia. Just stand at a corner on any busy street and observe closely the looks on people's faces. Anhedonia is written on almost every one of them.

> Despite having more sources of pleasure than ever before in history, we are probably the unhappiest people who have ever lived.

THE CAUSES OF MODERN ANHEDONIA

There is no doubt in my mind that the anhedonia many of us are experiencing today is unlike anything our grandparents experienced. Modern anhedonia is different. It feels different. It looks different. And it has many different causes.

That anhedonia can have many causes is important to understand if you are going to build a healthy pleasure system. Understanding its more common causes will point you to some of the ways you can protect yourself, and those you love, from it.

There are at least five ways in which the pathways to the pleasure center of our brain can be disrupted.

Major Depression

Major depression, often caused by genetic factors or stress, can cause severe interruption of our pleasure system. In fact, anhedonia is one of the main symptoms we look for when diagnosing clinical depression. Bipolar disorder, in which depression alternates with severe mania or a state of extreme euphoria (not to be confused with pleasure) also falls into this category.

These depressions always produce profound anhedonia— the total absence of any interest in normally exciting activities. There is no joyfulness, and often you just wish you would die.

> Prolonged and intense stress can cause not only depression, but it can also cause anhedonia by directly overstimulating the pleasure circuits.

Mothers take no pleasure in their newborn babies, rose-lovers remain unmoved by some new variation, and the most ardent sports fan feels nothing when his favorite team wins the championship.

Since antidepressants are very effective in treating these forms of depression, you should seek treatment immediately. The longer you wait, the more resistant to treatment your depression will become, and your life will be a prolonged state of profound anhedonia.

Stress-Induced Depression and Anxiety

Prolonged and intense stress can cause not only depression, but it can also cause anhedonia by directly overstimulating the pleasure circuits. As I mentioned earlier, such overstimulation is called dopamine flooding because the brain chemical (neurotransmitter) that carries the pleasure message to the pleasure center is dopamine. The pursuit of highly stimulating, adrenaline-driven activity in work and play overloads our pleasure center and diminishes the pleasure response in our brain.

Since stress is the primary cause of depression and anhedonia, the solution is to learn the skills of de-stressing. Stress management counseling is imperative.

Addictions

Addictions operate by hijacking the pleasure system. They take the pleasure circuits captive to such an extent that nothing else can get a message to your pleasure system—only the addicting substance or behavior. That's why many drugs and behaviors are addicting. They displace all other pleasures except their own. They are so effective in delivering pleasure that other life events, which normally would offer pleasure in the absence of the addiction, can't get a show-in.

Recovery from any addiction is, in effect, a process whereby you recover the brain's pleasure system and open it up again to ordinary pleasures. I'll have more to say about this later.

Overstimulation of the Pleasure Center

Of all the causes of anhedonia, overstimulation of the brain's pleasure center is the one I am primarily focusing on in this book. It is the most neglected cause of anhedonia, by both parents and scientists, and the most pervasive. And overstimulation of the brain's pleasure center has the potential to do as much damage as addiction to any major drug.

> Overstimulation of the brain's pleasure center has the potential to do as much damage as addiction to any major drug.

The overstimulation of our pleasure system, as now being experienced through many high-tech gadgets, computers, games, iPods, and so on, actually creates what is called an addiction process—a process that slowly shuts down the brain's pleasure system like a regular addiction. I will examine this aspect of anhedonia in more detail later.

Disease States

Many physical and mental disorders, including schizophrenia, can severely impact our pleasure system, resulting in anhedonia. This is because they disrupt the biochemistry of the brain that delivers pleasure. Don't be surprised, then, to find that when you have the flu, your capacity to experience pleasure is diminished. In fact, the next time you get the flu, pay particular attention to how it affects your pleasure response. I suspect that an illness robbing us of pleasure is our body's way of slowing down so that healing can take place.

ANHEDONIA AS THE *NOTHING* FEELING

Not only does anhedonia have many causes, but it can also take many forms. Let's take a brief look at some of these.

In the bipolar disorder field, anhedonia has often been described as the *nothing* feeling, which is a very accurate representation. Those who suffer from bipolar disorder describe it as feeling emotionally numb. One is devoid of any pleasant or unpleasant feelings—both have been shut down. Sadly, the absence of feelings remains for some time even after the bipolar state has lifted and can even still be felt in the middle of a manic state.

It's difficult for normal people to understand the nothing feeling in someone who is manic because it sounds contradictory to the whirlwind manic state. One manic sufferer describes it like this: "Imagine you're being tossed about in a bitterly cold storm on the high seas. Now imagine you have forgotten your hat, waterproof mittens, and boots.

You are bitterly cold, teeth chattering, with goose bumps all over. You endure this for a while, but sooner or later you become immune to the cold. Your hands and feet go numb. You can't feel anything. Your mind might pound off the walls of your head like chunks of ice coming off your windshield. Your concentration is shot; you are nervous and jumpy, shivering to keep warm."

Another sufferer offered the following description: "The worst part of the nothing feeling is that the sufferer can't understand it. The mind is a jangled wreck. Your brain freezes over as if in an emotional ice age. You fear it is going to take a long time to thaw out."

This is the nothing feeling of anhedonia.

ANHEDONIA AS A DIFFERENT KIND OF SADNESS

Depression has been previously seen to be a form of sadness. When you are depressed you cry easily. You are not just unhappy but downright gloomy and miserable. But now we are increasingly seeing a different kind of depression where the dominant symptom is not sadness but *pleasurelessness*—or anhedonia. This form of depression is called *nonsadness depression*.

A sufferer of nonsadness depression does not feel the classic symptoms of melancholy but more a loss of zest for life. You don't necessarily feel lacking in energy, but you just don't want to do anything because you don't have any interest in doing

> We are increasingly seeing a different kind of depression where the dominant symptom is not sadness but pleasurelessness.

anything. In cases like this, it is probably the *reward* component that is missing. Your brain has lost the ability to reward your activities with a sense of pleasure.

ANHEDONIA AS A DIFFERENT KIND OF BOREDOM

I can recall feeling bored as a teenager a lot of the time. I grew up in South Africa, where there was not a lot of activity going on outside of school. Long summer holidays were spent throwing stones at make-believe enemies or stealing the neighbor's fruit when it got dark. There were no miniature radios or cassette players. Radios were expensive and bulky, and radio stations played mainly classic music, as there were no commercial stations except on shortwave radios. When television was finally invented, it didn't come to South Africa because the strict Reformed government banned it, believing it would corrupt our values. So my values were preserved, but I was still bored a lot.

> Many teenagers and even young children today cannot tolerate doing nothing for more than thirty seconds, max—then they demand more stimulation.

Today we are experiencing a different kind of boredom. Teenagers are bored, not because there is nothing to do, as in my day, but because they are overstimulated. Despite the phenomenal array of gadgets that can feed them entertainment twenty-four hours a day in every conceivable place, many teenagers feel bored most of the time. My boredom was due to not having enough stimulating activity in my life, but teenagers today are often bored because they are overstimulated. Their pleasure centers are saturated, so they cannot experience simple pleasures anymore. Quite a difference. Many teenagers and even young children today cannot tolerate doing nothing for more than thirty seconds, max—then they demand more stimulation.

Our local newspaper recently reported that a group of teens in a respectable neighborhood had stolen Nativity scenes from a number of local churches. In all, they had stolen twenty-seven baby Jesus statues and were planning to burn them. When caught and asked why they had robbed the Nativity scenes, they replied that they had acted out of boredom.

Stories like this don't surprise me one bit. Teenagers today have such a high level of stimulation—from continuous iPod or other MP3 player gadgets to satellite radio stations and perpetually active cell phones—that their pleasure centers are already totally dysfunctional. And they still have fifty or sixty more years of a bored and pleasureless life to go.

ANHEDONIA AS A FORM OF APATHY

Another form of anhedonia is commonly called apathy. If you don't know what apathy feels like, then count yourself fortunate. Apathy seems so close to anhedonia that some researchers claim that they are highly related, the one possibly causing the other.

What does apathy feel like? Here are some quotes from apathy sufferers:

* It feels like someone has pulled the plug and all your power has been shut off. You move as if it would take a bulldozer to shift you.

* Other people laugh while you grimace at what gives them amusement.

* Days are long, and you're thankful when you finally get to fall into an unmade bed. But getting up in the morning can be hell all over again.

Apathy is an *I don't care* feeling. You have no interest in what used to give you great joy. You can't get as much done each day as before. You

SIGNS OF UNHEALTHY APATHY

We all feel some signs of apathy from time to time, perhaps after a period of intense activity or excitement, or when our immune system is battling an invading virus. Occasionally, apathy may serve a protective purpose as it slows us down so that our body can heal itself.

But when is apathy out of bounds, indicating a more serious problem?

The following signs should be heeded if persistently present:

- You are no longer interested in activities you used to enjoy.
- You are neglecting your personal care and grooming.
- Someone else has to tell you to do things you used to do yourself.

eschew new experiences and avoid anything that takes a little extra effort to accomplish. And you can't even get excited when something really good comes along. Apathetic people are indifferent and spiritless as they shuffle through their chaotic lives, not caring that they don't care.

I found a story on the Internet, posted by a person named Andrea, that describes a state of apathy very well:

I am so lethargic and cannot find any way out . . . I cannot seem to make myself do anything. All I want or seem to be able to do to get out of bed is get the newspaper and try and read it, smoke, or open a can of something or eat a box of ice cream, watch TV or surf the Internet. And now [I have] a new addiction—buying things on e-Bay! Getting expensive!!! . . . I've gained forty pounds, don't care about my appearance, can't clean the house . . . and can't feel any excitement about seeing loved ones, can't think of anything or anwhere I want to be but in my bedroom.[1]

Sounds and feels a bit like depression, doesn't it? In some cases it might well be. But many experts argue that apathy is *not* always depression. How is apathy different than depression? Depression heightens your emotions. Your sadness feels sadder; your despair drives you crazy because it hurts so much. But in apathy, your emotions are severely blunted. You can't feel anything—even your depression.

So while severe apathy has many outward signs that mimic depression, inwardly there is something different going on. It doesn't show the emotional pain that depression does. Apathy is more likely to be a result of anhedonia, causing you not only to have a numbing of your pleasure center but also a numbing of your emotions.

So what causes the sort of apathy I am describing here? Pretty much the same things that cause

- You no longer want to get together with friends, as it is too much trouble.
- You prefer to stay in your pajamas all day.
- When something really good happens, you cannot get excited.
- You are less concerned about your personal problems than you used to be.
- You no longer care what happens to you, or if you live or die.
- You don't want to cook or even buy food for yourself.
- You cannot complete anything you start doing anymore.

If you or anyone close to you has more than two of these signs, you need to explore further why you are apathetic and possibly seek professional help. While apathy can be a sign of anhedonia, it may also mimic depression or indicate a more serious disorder.

anhedonia. Among the factors that have been identified is our society's orientation toward entertainment. We have become a nation of observers watching with increasing enthusiasm as the sensationalism of the show intensifies. Whether it's a reality show, primetime drama, or a presidential debate, if there is nothing sensational or extreme, then ratings plummet.

Even rock legend Pete Townsend warns that music downloads on the Internet are creating what he calls *listener apathy* in a generation of people who do not seriously appreciate songs or musical performance. As one music psychologist describes it, "The accessibility of music has meant that it is taken for granted and does not require a deep emotional commitment once associated with music appreciation." Pity the next generation of teenagers.

In summary, the addictive process that drives our world today not only robs us of pleasure but also takes away the energy we need to pursue things that can bring meaningful enjoyment. We need to heed the changes that are slowly taking place in the human brain.

> The addictive process that drives our world today not only robs us of pleasure but also takes away the energy we need to pursue things that can bring meaningful enjoyment.

If this all sounds very depressing, let me hasten to add that we don't have to sit around waiting for the mental health world to get its act together here. Some studies and clinical experience are showing that a person can recover from anhedonia by a change in lifestyle that lowers dependence on high states of excitement, accompanied by a good dose of some healthy cognitive therapy (much of which is contained in the second part of this book) as well as certain medications, particularly those that help to restore our pleasure system.

NOT ALL PLEASURE IS BIOLOGICAL

Since a lot of what is pleasurable to us has to be learned, it is an error to think that all pleasure comes purely from biological mechanisms. While the pleasure system is biological, it is controlled by higher parts of the brain—mechanisms that are learned. Not all pleasure is instinctive. Like so many aspects of the human brain, much of it is programmable. Unlike lower forms of life that rely very much on inbuilt, instinctive controls, the human brain is so highly developed that its programmable outer layer, called the cortex, is capable of overriding any residual instinctive mechanisms.

> Not all pleasure is instinctive. Like so many aspects of the human brain, much of it is programmable.

Take sex, for example. In animals, sex is not controlled by intimacy, as in humans. Animals don't have to build close relationships. For them, sex is a purely biological, pleasure-driven response. They don't have to think about it. No fantasies can help it on its way. But in humans, the cortex, or programmable part of the brain, *is* the primary sex organ. Simply put: what you *think* can open up or shut down sexual desire as easily as sunlight can open or shut a daisy.

Now this has major implications for how our pleasure system works—and how it can easily go astray. True, some things give us pleasure because of inbuilt mechanisms in our brain. These instincts act as reward mechanisms to ensure that we will do the right things in order to go on living. If, for instance, you become very thirsty while on a hiking trip and suddenly come upon a stream with cool, running water, the desire to plunge your face into that stream and drink that water will be so overwhelming and the experience so pleasurable that you'll stop everything else to enjoy it. But because our cortex, that part of the brain that is a blank slate at birth and has to learn and make connections before it can function, is so large and powerful, it also has to learn what should and shouldn't give us pleasure.

Not everything our pleasure system learns to associate with pleasure is healthy. Some of it can be unhealthy; it can be downright evil and self-destructive. For instance, a gang member may feel enormous euphoria when he snuffs out the life of a fellow gang member. But that is an ill-conceived pleasure. The pleasure system is doing what it is designed to do, but its programming has gone wrong. It is this *bad* programming that underlies many of our social problems today. I call them misguided pleasures. While this type of bad programming does not destroy our pleasure system, it misdirects our search for healthy pleasure and ultimately shuts down those higher values that add meaning to our basic pleasures. And this can be as devastating as the greatest addiction.

MEASURING YOUR ANHEDONIA

We now come to the most important part of this chapter. I have no doubt that some of the questions on your mind at this point are *How can I tell if my brain's pleasure system is normal? What are the signs of anhedonia and how can I measure it?*

Here is a test you can take to measure your level of anhedonia. Remember, your level of anhedonia can change from day to day. It will be affected by unpleasant experiences in your life. What you are measuring here is how you feel at the time you take the test. You need to evaluate whether or not this is how you feel generally.

TEST FOR ANHEDONIA

Definition

Anhedonia refers to the loss of capacity to experience pleasure or the inability to gain pleasure from normally pleasurable experiences.

Instructions

Use the following scale to enter a score for each question:

0 = Never or rarely

1 = Occasionally (I seem to be able to control it)

2 = Often (several times a week)

3 = Always (every day, and for a lot of the time)

Score

1. I used to enjoy good food but no longer do. _____

2. My emotions feel numb and I cannot respond to happy events. _____

3. Feelings of sadness can easily overwhelm me. _____

4. Other people now seem to be much happier than I am. _____

5. I have great difficulty trying to get going in the morning. _____

6. I have lost interest in activities that used to give me pleasure. _____

7. I cannot think of anything that can make me feel happy. _____

8. I cannot give or receive affection as well as I used to. _____

9. I feel that God is very far away and not interested in me. _____

10. I no longer want to socialize with people. _____

11. I avoid going to church, club, or other social activities. _____

12. I used to derive a lot of pleasure in hobbies or creative activities but no longer do. _____

13. Even when I accomplish something significant, I cannot enjoy it. _____

14. Most of what is happening in my life bores me, and only *big* things can excite me. _____

15. The worst time of the day for me is the morning or after I have taken a nap. _____

Total _____

Scoring and Interpretation

Total the score given to each question. The highest possible score is 45.

  0 to 7: Your score is low and reflects little or no anhedonia.

 8 to 15: There might be some mild, temporary anhedonia in some areas of your life.

16 to 20: Your score is beginning to show some moderate anhedonia that might be troubling in some areas of your life.

21 to 25: You are showing some high signs of anhedonia—if it is not temporary, you may need to get some help for it. Rule out depression.

26 to 30: Your anhedonia is high enough to clearly warrant professional help. You may be clinically depressed.

31 to 35: Your anhedonia is severe and needs professional help.

Over 36: Your anhedonia is very severe and needs immediate professional help.

LEVELS OF ANHEDONIA

Anhedonia is not an all-or-nothing phenomenon. Rather, there are gradations of severity, starting at a perfectly healthy pleasure system and increasing to a level that can only be described as pathological because it is so severe that the pleasure system in the brain has totally shut down.

An example of the pathological level would be a very serious depression or schizophrenia in which nothing, and I mean *nothing*, can give the slightest bit of pleasure. If such a disordered person would also be, say, a cocaine addict, the craving for cocaine would also be absent. Even in the severest of addictions, the pleasure system, while blocked to outside origins of pleasure, can still create a craving for the addicted substance. The problem is not that there is no pleasure capacity but rather that the pleasure system is being held hostage to the addictive substance.

> If you have concerns about how little you can extract pleasure from your life, seek out some counseling.

Between these two extremes, there are several levels of anhedonia, starting at the mild level, where the system is only slightly blocked, increasing in severity to where it is being hijacked by major sources of pleasure, both good and bad.

No matter where you score on the anhedonia scale, if you have concerns about how little pleasure you can extract from your life, seek out some counseling. Life is too short and precious to waste on anhedonia.

PLEASURE AND HEDONISM

Before closing this chapter, I want to address my Christian readers specifically. No doubt some of you are uncomfortable with my use of the term *pleasure*. Conservative believers generally have a very negative view of pleasure because historically it has been associated with what the apostle Paul refers to as *the flesh* and connotes hedonism, which is seeking after pleasure for pleasure's sake.

Obviously, I am not using the term *pleasure* in a hedonistic sense. Hedonism is an ugly thing. Hedonism is narcissistic, self-centered, and has no place for God. It pursues pleasure to the neglect of everything else in life. However, there is a normal and healthy pleasure that comes from your brain, is part of nature's design, and is not hedonistic. Believers want to be able to take pleasure in God. Is this hedonistic? Obviously not. God wants us to take pleasure in Him.

> Moderate, healthy pleasure . . . will always be the source of genuine happiness.

So how does one tell the difference between good pleasure and selfish, hedonistic pleasure? The answer is simple: hedonistic pleasure eventually leads to anhedonia. This should be clear from everything I have said this far.

Moderate, healthy pleasure—the sort of pleasure that comes from ordinary, everyday, simple experiences of life and does not require a thrill or high level of excitement—will always be the source of genuine happiness because these joys are the basic building blocks of authentic happiness. And this is what the next chapter is all about.

PLEASURE OR HAPPINESS?

But pleasures are like poppies spread,
you seize the flow'r, its bloom is shed;
Or like the snow falls in the river,
A moment white—then melts for ever.
—ROBERT BURNS, "TAM O' SHANTER"

Time magazine published a Special Mind and Body Issue in 2005: The Science of Happiness. In an article entitled "The Biology of Joy," it was reported that a prominent brain researcher had discovered that happiness, an essential emotion in pleasure, "isn't just a vague, ineffable feeling [but] a physical state of the brain." Furthermore, it is possible to deliberately induce such a state of happiness.[1] In every sense of the idea, therefore, happiness is a choice. You can have it or not—it's your choice.

HAPPINESS AFFECTS THE WHOLE BODY

But that's not all. As researchers have learned more and more about the healthy brain's pleasure-producing mechanisms, they have also discovered that these traits have a powerful influence on the rest of the body. Happy people, meaning those whose pleasure circuits were in good shape, developed 50 percent more antibodies than average in response to flu vaccines. Pleasure also helps to boost related mental states, such as hopefulness, optimism, and contentment, and it lowers incidences of heart disease, diabetes, hypertension, colds and upper-respiratory infections. Quite a remarkable emotion. Clearly, nature intends us to have well-functioning pleasure and happiness circuits if we want to live hale and hearty lives.

> While the health of your pleasure system is central to everything you enjoy, pleasure itself should not be the sole focus of a meaningful life.

There is also a strong belief that the pleasure you take in life (generalized happiness) is the accumulation of the pleasure derived from many aspects of your life. To place too much reliance on just one particular source of pleasure probably means your total accumulation of pleasure (happiness) won't be as great as if you could spread the source of pleasure around a bit more. It also appears that your sum of pleasure in life can be reduced by negative feelings such as worry or exhaustion. Reducing these negatives can, therefore, contribute a lot to building greater happiness.

But my bottom line here is this: while the health of your pleasure system is central to everything you enjoy, pleasure itself should not be the sole focus of a meaningful life.

The pleasures we experience are like railway stations along a long journey. They are short stops that infuse our life with fulfilling enjoyment, but then the train has to move on to the next part of our journey. The great Scottish poet Robert Burns was right: pleasure is just "a moment white—then melts forever."

But don't underestimate the importance of these short moments of pleasure. In the setting of the larger journey of our life, these *pleasure stops* provide the building blocks for enduring happiness.

HOW ARE PLEASURE AND HAPPINESS DIFFERENT?

Most experts believe that happiness and pleasure are not the same thing— and I agree up to a point. While the average person tends to believe that people can buy happiness through money and hard work, it is really only pleasure that they are buying. Whether this pleasure becomes happiness or not is another matter. It takes something extra to turn pleasure into happiness.

While pleasure is not the same as happiness, you cannot experience the feeling of happiness if your pleasure center has been hijacked. I believe that this explains why so many people today are not happy. They lack a healthy pleasure system—in other words, they are anhedonic. And without a healthy pleasure system, they cannot feel any happiness. Or to put it even more simply, you need a healthy pleasure system to be able to enjoy that which is trying to make you happy.

> You can only be really happy if you preserve the functioning of your pleasure system.

This is what happiness is all about. To be happy, you need to be able to appreciate the good things in your life. So pleasure is not happiness, but you can only be really happy if you preserve the functioning of your pleasure system.

THE HEDONIC TREADMILL

In a recent article in the *Monitor on Psychology*, a psychologist recalls how she was almost blind until just a few years ago. Then she had LASIK eye surgery, and for the first time since she was twelve years old, she could see perfectly.

As you can imagine, she was ecstatic. "Miraculous," she called it. She had never been this happy. But after just one week, her elation faded. She was stunned, but it illustrates the brain's ability to quickly adjust to both positive and negative changes in the pleasure system.[2]

It is this tendency of the brain to get used to everything that feels good that causes many to jump on what is called the *hedonic treadmill*, where they are continually seeking out short-term mood boosters to give them temporary moments of pleasure. In the long run, the hedonic treadmills shuts down our pleasure system by forcing us to keep finding things that are even more exciting to give us pleasure. In effect, this is an addictive process that makes it hard for us to achieve any sense of enduring happiness if we don't keep it under control.

THE REDISCOVERY OF HAPPINESS

Much has been written about happiness in recent times, but most of it is not helpful or doesn't make sense when you consider that whereas the brain has a specific center for delivering pleasure, it has no such locus for happiness. It seems that happiness is a function of the whole brain, not just one part of it.

Philosophy hasn't helped that much. Mostly it warns us that happiness is a fragile thing. According to Wilfred McClay, happiness is fertile and mysterious, something that comes in many sizes and colors and shapes.[3] The more self-conscious and obsessed we are in pursuing happiness, the more dissatisfied and unhappy we become. Mostly, happiness is a matter of having the right expectations. This makes a lot of sense. The unhappiest people I know all have unrealistic expectations for their lives. Also, it seems that our happiness is keenest in times when we can recollect earlier happy times. This is such an important point that it is the basis of the exercises I will describe later.

Until recently, psychology hasn't been of much help either. For a long time, psychologists ignored or even ridiculed the emotion of happiness on the grounds that it was too subjective and impossible to measure. That has now changed, and many psychologists are scrambling to find ways to help people achieve a higher level of genuine happiness. It is no longer politically incorrect to mention happiness in psychological circles, I'm pleased to report, having once written a book on the topic myself when the topic was being ridiculed.[4]

Many people confuse pleasure with happiness and spend their lives trying to pump as much pleasure into their existence as they possibly can, hoping that it will make them happy. Patently, this is a lost cause. So what I want to do in this chapter is show how you can make a healthier connection between your pleasure and happiness. It is very easy to look for happiness in all the wrong places, when it is right under your nose in your inbuilt ability to experience pleasure.

But before we continue our discussion of happiness, let's take a little test that will help us to tell the difference between pleasure and happiness.

MEASURING PLEASURE AND HAPPINESS

Instructions

Imagine that the following events are possible in your life, and answer the following questions by circling T if it is generally true or F if it is generally false.

I feel great delight whenever . . .

1. I get a gift or present from someone of something I want.   T / F
2. A friend I haven't seen for a long time comes to visit.   T / F
3. I buy myself a new item of clothing or a gadget I've wanted.   T / F
4. I am at home, quietly reading a book or watching TV with my family.   T / F
5. I am on my way to a fantastic vacation.   T / F
6. I do a good deed that was unselfish, even if it was not appreciated.   T / F
7. I go to the movies or a sports game I've been looking forward to.   T / F
8. I walk through a park where children are playing.   T / F
9. I have completed a major task that has taken me quite a while to finish.   T / F
10. I visit a sick elderly person who is being neglected by his/her family.   T / F

Add up the True responses you have given to the odd-numbered items.   _____

Then add up the number of True responses to the even-numbered items.   _____

Did you take the Measuring Pleasure and Happiness test? If so, you should have two scores. The first is the number of True responses to the odd-numbered items (somewhere between 0 and 5), and the second is the number of True responses for the even-numbered items (also somewhere between 0 and 5). Now let's see what this means.

The number of True responses to the odd-numbered items essentially measures your *pleasure*. It is indicative of the delight that you get from the external events in your life—things you receive or do that give you pleasure. A normal person will probably score a full 5 on this short test, provided his pleasure center is working properly.

> All pleasure sooner or later loses its capacity to make us happy.

Now let's look at the second score—for the even-numbered items. These items relate to *happiness*. The score also ranges from 0 to 5, but my guess is that not too many of you scored a perfect 5. It wouldn't surprise me if you only scored a zero.

YOUR PLEASURE SCORE

Let's first examine your pleasure score (the total of odd-numbered items). Pleasure is the enjoyment that comes from what is happening to you on the outside—pleasurable life events that make your world go round. And these things do make you feel happy to a certain extent. Quite obviously, these delights send signals along the dopamine pathways to the pleasure center in your brain, and that's why you enjoy them. But they are pleasures, not true happiness. They are pleasures that might help you to feel happy for a while—but only for as long as they provide pleasure.

And as we all know, even the most stimulating and fantastic new event that comes along can only give short-term pleasure before the feeling fades away as you get used to it. In other words, *all* pleasure sooner or later loses its capacity to make us happy. This is not to say that we no longer value these kinds of pleasures. However, all pleasure by design is temporary. Sooner or later, our pleasure system adjusts to

> True happiness is more enduring than pleasure.

what is giving you pleasure and then goes back to wait for the next pleasure surprise.

YOUR HAPPINESS SCORE

Now let's examine your happiness score (the total of even-numbered items). Happiness does not depend on glitzy, pleasure-filled experiences. It comes more from a feeling of deep contentment or the appreciation of the finer things of your life. Happiness is not a flash-in-the-pan experience, nor does it fade away easily. All we have to do to recapture happiness is to remember what we can be happy about—deep friendships, the joy of doing someone a favor, and the appreciation of love and kindness. These joys come more from the *reward* part of the pleasure center, not its flashy pleasure part.

What is important to notice here is that true happiness is more enduring than pleasure. Please keep in mind, however, that the pleasure circuits in the brain are still extremely important. As I have already indicated, some ability to feel pleasure is essential to a happy life. Happiness must have connections to the pleasure system. But don't think you can raise your general happiness level just by cramming all the pleasure you can into your life—which is what so many are doing today, only to find themselves feeling unsatisfied and numb.

EXPLORING THE DIFFERENCES FURTHER

Everyone wants to be happy. I know I want to be happy, which is why the topic has intrigued me throughout my career as a psychologist. After having written several books on the topic of depression, I finally got up the courage to write a book on happiness.[5]

At the time I wrote *15 Principles for Achieving Happiness*, the topic of happiness was suspect. Awkwardly, happiness had a sort of negative connotation in psychology and theology circles—a sort of cynicism prevailed. It was a topic best left to an episode of *Oprah* or self-help gurus, not professionals. Pastors used to challenge me with, "But isn't it selfish, even sinful, to try to increase your happiness? After all, most of the world lives in poverty while the other half suffers from self-indulgence." Thanks to Sigmund Freud, who invented the *pleasure principle* (the idea that the pursuit of pleasure is what the "child in us" obsesses about), being miserable was about as high a level of happiness most Christians, and others, aspired to.

Thankfully, this attitude has now changed. Today happiness is big business. It is considered to be such an important buffer to mental illness that even Ivy League schools are now offering graduate-level courses on the topic of happiness and how to achieve it.

WHAT IS HAPPINESS?

But we are still left with a vexing question. What is happiness? This is a tough question to answer. It depends on to whom you talk. What fascinates me is that we all think we know what happiness is, since we all know the feeling of happiness. Yet scientists still have great difficulty trying to determine what happiness is. There is no brain signature to identify it. Even more difficult is to figure out how to produce happiness in oneself. If someone were to invent a real happy pill, he or she would make a fortune.

So let me have a try. Basically, happiness is both a state of mind and a way of life. It is a feeling, no doubt about that. But it is also a state of well-being characterized by other emotions, ranging from contentment to intense joy. So happiness is not an all-or-nothing experience; it comes in many levels and types.

One type, for me at least, is the happiness I experience in the evenings when, at the end of a busy day, my wife and I sit on our family room couch with our dog, Andy, nestled between us. We read or watch a favorite British comedy on TV. I often remark to my wife that this happiness is *heavenly*, to which my wife will respond, "Honey, I'm sure heaven is even better than this." Maybe. But I'd settle for this happiness quite easily.

Another type of happiness I recently experienced was watching my grandchildren graduate from high school and seeing the joy on my grandson's face when he turned twenty-one. So happiness comes in many sizes and for a variety of reasons. The most immediate type of happiness arises when you have a feeling of joy or pleasure at, say, meeting a friend or completing a task. But we can also experience happiness through being aware that life is satisfying, without having any immediate experience of a *high* feeling. Just remembering some of the good things that have happened to us—a prize we won, the birth of a child, or something you are grateful for—can make us very happy.

INCREASE YOUR HAPPINESS AWARENESS EXERCISE

People usually don't attend to their feelings of happiness—not until it is taken away. Happy feelings are not as intrusive as unhappy ones. So a good starting point would be for you to try to become more aware of your happy feelings, so that they never go unnoticed.

I am *not* implying that one should be happy all the time. Heaven forbid! Perpetual happiness will destroy your capacity for it. But knowing when something makes you happy is the essence of gratefulness, which, as we will see later, can actually increase your general level of happiness.

So try this Increase Your Happiness Awareness exercise:

* Carry a small card with you through the day.

* Then about every hour, try to evaluate your level of happiness on a scale of zero to ten, zero being the unhappiest you have ever been, five for average happiness, and ten for the highest level of happiness you have ever experienced.

* Also make a note alongside each, rating what it is that you think is making you happy or unhappy at that time.

* Keep these cards, one for each day, as you continue reading this book so you can see how your score changes as you begin to uncover new strategies for healthy emotional living.

WHAT ROBS US OF HAPPINESS?

Happy people are wonderful to be around. Their happiness is contagious because it helps to open up our happiness pathways. Happy people engender a sense of security because they seem to be safer than unhappy people.

According to a number of studies that have been conducted around the world, the desire for happiness is second only to the desire for health and a long life. No surprise there. However, what is astounding is that happiness is ranked more important than sex, having a good job, wealth, status, and being a celebrity. If you compare different persons, cultures, religions, ages, gender, and races, happiness rankings do not vary much. It seems that there is a universal desire to be happy.

But these same studies have come up with a disquieting bit of reality: most of the people surveyed report that they are in fact unhappy most of the time. Money, for instance, does not seem to add much happiness, once you have reached the minimum needed to survive. It would be ridiculous to suggest that people who are starving couldn't be a little happier if they had enough money to take away the feelings that accompany starvation. What seem to be prime determiners of happiness all revolve around relationships: a good marriage, an abundance of close friends, and lots of time in fellowship and socializing. What alarms me is that many people report that their children don't bring joy. This is hard for me to appreciate when I reflect on my own children, who are a source of much of my happiness—although to be honest, raising children can sometimes be a source of much pain.

YOUR HAPPINESS SET POINT

Many of the things people think could make them happy, if only they could get enough, turn out to be no guarantee for happiness. For instance, having sex more frequently, being rich or powerful, living a life of ease, or accomplishing some great thing with your life, all turn out not to make a lot of difference to your happiness level. Happiness, it appears, comes from little things, such as good friendships, a harmonious family life, a fulfilling vocation, good health, and a tranquil mind. And high stress is almost certainly going to torpedo and sink these little ships.

This brings us to a very basic reality about happiness: just as our weight has a set point, so that even after the most arduous dieting you will almost certainly end up back at that nasty bit of flab, scientists are saying that we also have a set point for happiness. Win the jackpot or achieve some great fame, be happy for a while, but then be prepared to end up where you began. Identical twins turn out always to be at about identical happiness levels, no matter how long they've been separated.

An important lesson in happiness comes from the lottery world. I suppose everybody secretly wants to win the lottery because they think that it would make them happy. Imagine not having to worry about your job or being broke. A fascinating report from the BBC in the UK looked at the effect of winning the lottery from around the world.[6] While initially lottery winners are caught up in a flood of euphoria, it quickly fades, leaving them feeling worse than before. In fact, most lottery winners return to their prewinning levels of happiness within a year. Many forfeit all happiness and end up miserable: "If I'd known what was going to transpire, honestly, I would have torn the ticket up!"

I believe that the reason is linked to the topic of this book. The sudden influx of cash literally hijacks the brain's pleasure center like an addiction to cocaine. After such euphoria, simple things no longer bring joy. The pleasure system is washed out. This can lead down a dark road to drugs, sex, and the pursuit of the euphoria that we once had. Bankruptcy and even death can result. Blissful prosperity is a myth and rarely ensues. It certainly cannot alter your happiness set point. Reason? The lottery is not about what one wins, but about what one loses. And few seem to get the balance right mainly because they do not understand how the brain delivers its pleasure—and hence its happiness.

But back to the ordinary lives of you and me. Having disabused you of any fantasies about wealth, and lest the prospect of having to live out your life at your present low level of happiness should make you even more unhappy, let me hasten to add this good news: with a little effort you can change your happiness set point. I know; I did. How did I accomplish this? Mainly through several of the exercises that I will present in the second part of this book. Just knowing that happiness is something you have some control over can go a long way to motivating your change.

Unhappiness does not come about by accident. There are usually actions and attitudes that create unhappiness. In fact, some actions will guarantee it. Scientists are in agreement here.

While happiness is more than mere pleasure, you cannot expect to be happy if you suffer from anhedonia. You need a healthy pleasure system to be able to experience happiness. However, it should already be obvious that the perpetual pursuit of pleasure actually works against the simple joys of happiness.

One way you can move up your happiness set point is to examine what you are neglecting in your quest for happiness.

Do you remember the song from *Camelot* that King Arthur and Guinevere sing when she is frustrated and cannot find any happiness, even though she has all the big things of her life lined up? The song is called "What Do the Simple Folk Do?" I have a particular fondness for the music from *Camelot*

> The perpetual pursuit of pleasure actually works against the simple joys of happiness.

because my youngest daughter starred as Guinevere in a Los Angeles production of the show some years ago. The words from that song express very clearly the point I am making here.

You will recall that Guinevere, feeling anhedonic I suspect, asks King Arthur what it is that simple folk do to help them escape when they're blue. His reply? He has been informed—by those who know them well—that they find relief in quite a clever way. When they're sorely pressed they whistle, and whistling seems to brighten up their day.

Guinevere, not satisfied with that answer, pushes King Arthur for more. He then adds three more options: a lad with a voice three times his size sings, some people dance a fiery dance, and others sit around and wonder what royal folk do.

I love it! What great words of wisdom. Real, deep, and abiding happiness doesn't come from the excitements of life but from the simple joys of plain living. And this is where unhappy people usually miss this boat.

NOW FOR THE BIG QUESTION

Why am I exploring with you the inner workings of happiness? It leads me to this supersized point: many of us are unhappy because we are abusing our pleasure system. Plain and simple.

This has major implications for how we are to live and for how we might change our happiness set point. Let me once again recall the main point of this chapter: you cannot achieve any measure of enduring happiness in your life unless your pleasure center is functioning properly. Or to put it another

> Many of us are unhappy because we are abusing our pleasure system.

way, if you interfere with your pleasure system, you will destroy your capacity for real, enduring happiness. To prove this point we need merely look at two disorders that we know can rob us of happiness by creating anhedonia.

The first is the problem of addiction. We know—and I will cover this in more detail in a later chapter—that addictions are addicting precisely because they abuse and hijack the pleasure center of the brain, producing a state of anhedonia. This means that only the substance or behavior that has become addicting is capable of creating pleasure. Gamblers gamble because that is the only way they can feel any sort of happiness. Cocaine abusers can only enjoy cocaine. It is their sole source of happiness. It stands to reason, therefore, that when access to the pleasure system of the brain is restricted to the addiction, the state of anhedonia that follows will block happy feelings related to anything else.

The second is the disorder of depression. Anhedonia is one of the cardinal symptoms of clinical depression. And depressed people are also unhappy. If a depressed person could be happy, he or she wouldn't be depressed. Here again we see a close connection between anhedonia and the lack of happiness. Like Jack and Jill, they go together. Never one without the other.

HOW DOES THIS RELATE TO ORDINARY PEOPLE?

But how does this all apply to normal, nonaddicted, respectable, church-going people? Unfortunately, more than we might think. Almost anyone can get caught up seeking ever-increasing pleasure without realizing just how subtle the process of anhedonia is. In my clinical practice, I have found that I spend more and more time teaching my patients to back off from a constant pursuit of special thrills.

> When you become content with ordinary feelings, you will find that they are more beautiful and far more satisfying than thrill-loaded experiences.

And I am talking about normal people—not perverts. Ordinary folks can easily get caught up in trying to enhance pleasure by engaging in unhealthy kinds of stimulation. This always leads to anhedonia.

Try to be content with ordinary experiences; don't keep looking for new sensations. And when you become content with ordinary feelings, you will find that they are more beautiful and far more satisfying than thrill-loaded experiences.

BUILDING HAPPINESS BY ENHANCING YOUR PLEASURE

Life is rich—it holds an abundant smorgasbord of healthy pleasures that can be pursued with gusto. There is no excuse to be miserable in this life. If we are, it is because we have chosen to neglect some important principles. We can spend our lives grudgingly keeping ourselves from enjoying legitimate pleasures, or we can free ourselves to be happy.

Two important happiness boosters for you to consider are work and hobbies. Some of life's greatest pleasures can be found in meaningful work. Permanent leisure will never

HAPPINESS BOOSTERS

1. Intentionally do something unselfish for someone else every day.
2. Give yourself permission to make mistakes and quickly forgive yourself.
3. Give up expecting others to be perfect—just accept them as they are.
4. Whenever anyone offends you, forgive him or her without delay.
5. Try to simplify your life—do a makeover from top to bottom.
6. Make sure you get enough sleep and exercise every day.
7. Spend as much time as you possibly can with those you love.
8. Spend twenty minutes each day in quiet reflection or meditation.
9. Each day, take a few minutes to write down all that worries you—

and then cross out the ones you have no control over.

10. Every night before going to sleep, remind yourself of five things you are grateful for.

Add others to the list as they come to mind. I am sure that with a little thought, you could easily add a few dozen really effective happiness boosters. This exercise will prepare you well for the next chapter, in which I will address what is perhaps the greatest destroyer of pleasure and happiness in our day—modern-day stress.

make us really happy, since work is as natural and necessary to life as eating and sleeping. "Wait until I retire," I hear many say in my consulting room. "Then I will be happy. Until then, I will just put up with the drudgery." Sad . . . and nonsense! Studies have already been done to show that meaningful work always enhances happiness.

Hobbies are also important. When one's work is drudgery, you can always make up for what is missing through hobbies. Being able to complete a creative task, no matter how small, universally produces pleasure. I love teaching people to be creative. Hobbies do not have to cost a lot of money. In fact, I would say if your hobby is expensive, it isn't a hobby. One can collect bits of nature for nothing. Take wildflowers, for example. On a recent trip to Switzerland, I collected samples of wildflowers, pressing each flower between the pages of a book. I brought them home as a gift to one of my daughters, who collects them. She was overjoyed. I could not have purchased a better gift.

Now that you have some idea of how you boost your pleasure system, I have prepared an additional list of happiness boosters you can work on. As I close this chapter, I invite you to work through the list and see how many you can add to your life.

STRESS AND ANHEDONIA

*Most men pursue pleasure with such breathless haste
that they hurry right past it.*
—SøREN KIERKEGAARD

The problem of stress has been coming on for a long time, so slow and insidious that we have not noticed how profoundly it has invaded our lives. It's hard to believe, but as far back as 1880, a man by the name of George Miller Beard tried to get the world's attention to something he called *nervousness*. He was a physician and neurologist from New York, after whom a disorder called *Beard's disease* was named. This term was used to describe persons with unexplained exhaustion and abnormal fatigability. Today we call it *stress*.

What was happening in the world at the time Beard started to raise awareness of stress? It was the advent of the steam train. Suddenly the pace of life picked up. People didn't have to walk or ride a horse; they could catch a train and have extra time to do more things.

Welcome to a new type of stress. Soon after came the automobile, and then the Wright brothers, then fast jets that could take you all the way across the United States in just a few hours, compared to the many days it took on a train—days that gave you plenty of time to rest.

Then came the telephone, radio, and television. And all these marvelous developments seemed so innocuous. But they were the harbingers of an even greater stress-inducing phenomenon—computers. These fantastic benefits, however, accelerated the pace of life, increased competitiveness, reduced rest and leisure time, and created a demand for greater output of nervous energy.

But that was only the beginning of the stress problem. Now, almost every aspect of modern life that we have come to depend upon, such as cell phones and the Internet, has increased the pace of life exponentially, and our stress is now going through the roof.

> Modern life is slowly pushing real pleasure further and further away from us.

The average person is stimulated and driven at such a pace today that the human body is frantically trying to adapt to this supercharged environment. These days, who has little to do? Who has nothing to worry about? Who doesn't feel exhausted a lot of the time? Who knows how to relax? (I mean really relax, not just vegetate in front of a TV.) Our schools, businesses, and churches are all sources of ruthless stress, and even stay-at-home moms are so extended and their life strings are so strung out they could reach a high C without moving a vocal finger.

And what is the penalty we pay? Healthy, positive pleasure is becoming more elusive. Modern life is slowly pushing real pleasure further and further away from us.

CAN STRESS BE GOOD FOR YOU?

We now live in a supertense world—tenser than it has ever been in history, primarily because we have lost recovery time. There used to be a lot of it, but now it's all but vanished.

We read and talk about tension all the time. Doctors often tell patients to relax, and articles about stress appear in many popular magazines. Yet while there was—for a short period a few decades ago—a high level of concern and awareness of how damaging stress is to physical and emotional health, most people today accept stress as a fact of life and prefer to live with it. In fact, the most popular type of book today is one that tries to convince you that stress is really something good for you and that you should even try to create more of it.

> In my opinion, the only good stress is that which is short-lived.

People desperately want reassurance that their hectic life is OK—that they are going down the right track. They don't want to be bothered with challenges to reduce their stress. The word *relax* is more often used to admonish someone who is aggravating them, rather than as gentle advice for a highly stressed-out friend.

Want my opinion? Hogwash! We are just trying to rationalize our stress. It's out of control, and no amount of rationalizing is helpful. Prolonged stress is killing us, and if it doesn't kill us physically, it kills our ability to experience real and abiding happiness.

I am emphasizing this point because I have noticed my patients becoming more and more resistant to getting help for lowering the stress in their lives. They push for help on how to live with their stress or perhaps want help in finding out how they can increase their tolerance for it. They prefer books that offer to turn stress into a positive factor in their lives, rather than books that encourage them to reduce stress. My books have always been the latter. In my opinion, the only good stress is that which is short-lived.

STRESS AND THE PLEASURE SYSTEM

What does losing the war against stress have to do with the loss of our pleasure? Simply this: stress robs us of our precious ability to experience pleasure. It is a major cause of anhedonia.

The mental and physiological changes that occur whenever we are under excessive or prolonged stress directly undermine important chemical messengers that the brain needs to function properly. These chemical messengers carry signals not only to all the major parts of the brain but to the heart of our pleasure center as well. Result? Depression and anxiety, and in their wake comes anhedonia.

The idea that stress can rob us of the ability to collect pleasure from daily activities may seem strange, even improbable to most readers. But it is a scientific fact. The effect of stress on our pleasure system has been extensively studied in both humans and animals.

> Stress robs us of our precious ability to experience pleasure.

One fascinating study is worth mentioning here because it clearly proves that stress and pleasure are not good companions. Two researchers in Basel, Switzerland, performed an interesting experiment using mice. It appears that mice have a particular fondness for sweet things—a sweet tooth, if you will—not unlike ourselves. They'll do almost anything to get some candy.

Using sucrose dissolved in water, the researchers first carefully measured how much of the sweet liquid a mouse normally drank over several days, so as to get a baseline of consumption that was a measure of the existing hedonic (pleasure) state of the mouse. Then in a very humane way, they began to apply some chronic, mild, unpredictable stress, the equivalent of what you and I experience daily—only scaled down to mouse size.

The results were most revealing. Over a two-week period, each mouse began to show a steady decrease in the consumption of the sucrose. The longer the stress remained in their lives, the more their pleasure system lost interest in sweet things. Stress was making the mice anhedonic.

Then the researchers began to vary the stress level, up or down. The pleasure system followed suit, going up when stress was lowered and going down when stress was raised. The good news was that at the end of the experiment when the researchers removed the stress, the mice all went back to guzzling the sucrose water at their former level.[1] Their pleasure systems had become hedonic again. No need to organize any protests against animal research here.

Even more amazing was that these findings have been validated using more sophisticated techniques. For instance, rather than using sucrose water, researchers used self-stimulation of electrodes implanted in an animal's brain. Each time the animal pressed a lever, it got a shot of pleasurable feelings, like the experiment I described in the first chapter. Animals under stress reduced their level of self-stimulation; their pleasure systems wouldn't respond even when they were stimulated directly.

STRESS ISN'T GOING AWAY

Chronic and prolonged stress turns off the pleasure system of all animals, including us complex humans. So if you are stressed out, don't be surprised if you are experiencing a high degree of anhedonia.

When I wrote my book *Adrenaline and Stress* nearly twenty years ago (before we had the Internet), the stress of modern life already seemed to be out of control. But as I reflect back on that time, today's stress seems to be even crazier. Any comparison seems ridiculous. It's a different world we face today.

From *Time* magazine to women's journals, articles expressing concern about stress abound. Frequently, psychiatry and neurology journals have something to say about it. And for good reason. Stress damage to the body and mind has reached a perplexing magnitude. The chronic stress of twenty-first-century living is not a mere inconvenience but a major problem that needs to be recognized and treated seriously, many experts are saying. Unless we, as a society, learn to slow down, examine our values, and change our hectic lifestyles, we will continue to suffer from cardiovascular disease, immune deficiencies, depression, and a host of other illnesses. Further, we will pass these traits and poor coping skills to our children.

> If you are stressed out, don't be surprised if you are experiencing a high degree of anhedonia.

Here is an example of how our children can be affected by stress. Peter came to see me because he realized something was out of kilter with his life. He had started having panic attacks (a stress-related disorder). As an attorney who had to commute to downtown Los Angeles, Peter's life had become more and more complicated as he became more successful. In his line of work, almost every day he encountered a crisis that had to be resolved. He started to have periodic dizzy spells (due to elevated blood pressure), and he ended every day with a severe headache (tension headaches usually occur when your adrenaline finally begins to drop, so after work ends).

But the reason Peter sought my counsel was not about his personal problems. His fourteen-year-old son had become morose and despondent. As I explored the circumstances, it appeared that Peter—a driven man—had become a driver for his son from an early age. The boy was exceptionally gifted intellectually. So Peter had insisted that the son go to a special private school where he could be driven to *super-succeed* (a favorite expression of Peter's). Each day the boy had to leave home very early in the morning to travel some distance to this school, arrive home late, and then put in several hours of homework.

Well, to cut a long story short, while the son had complied with his dad's push to succeed to the best of his ability, one day he refused to get out of bed. It wasn't that he didn't want to get out of bed; he felt incapable of getting out of bed. Peter panicked, not knowing whether his son was faking the cop-out or whether something had gone wrong.

Something had gone wrong. Capable as the boy was, the pressure and stress of his life triggered a severe depression. Overloaded, his system just switched off. Anhedonia and energy depletion took over.

I instigated the appropriate treatment for the son and then sat down to confront the father. Despite Peter's good intentions, he was wrecking his son's life. The son was doing everything he could to please his father, a typical example of the warning that experts are screaming out loud and clear: our children could experience even greater suffering given their exposure to severe stress from the first days of life.

STRESS AND PLEASURE DON'T MIX

You don't have to be a rocket scientist to figure out that stress and pleasure don't get on well together. Just look within yourself. Are the happiest moments of your life those when you have been under the greatest stress? Obviously not. The stress response—also known as the *fight-or-*

flight response—has as its sole purpose helping us survive whatever crisis we are facing. How happy you feel in the fight-or-flight mode of your body is of no concern to your brain. Survival is all that matters.

In a sense, pleasure and stress are mutually exclusive—the one displaces the other. But there is some good news here that is often overlooked. The connection between the two is not a one-way street, with stress destroying pleasure, as you might imagine. Yes, stress does undermine our pleasure system as I will show in a short while. But the redeeming news is that the pursuit of the right sort of pleasure, what I call *natural* pleasure, can be a powerful antidote for stress.

Natural pleasure is the pleasure that comes from the moderate use of our inbuilt senses such as taste, thirst, touch, or creative satisfaction. When you sit on a hillside watching a beautiful sunset, contemplating the beauty of God's creation, you are allowing your pleasure system to play the game it knows best—giving you pleasure naturally. And this form of pleasure lowers your stress level. Guaranteed!

> The pursuit of the right sort of pleasure, what I call natural pleasure, can be a powerful antidote for stress.

A recent news report claims that when it comes to our senses (taste, sound, touch, smell, and sight) generally we have no sense.[2] Modern anhedonia and overuse of our senses have frozen them out. We gulp down our food without really tasting it, blast our iPods so we don't really hear music, and generally can't see or feel the forest for the trees.

There is unequivocal evidence that creating simple joy through such activities as spending time with a real friend, your children or grandchildren, or being creative through a hobby can significantly lower your cortisol level. And cortisol, a stress hormone released from your adrenal glands, is one of the major players in the stress game. It's your ally at the start of your stress episode, but if stress hangs around too long (usually longer than two weeks), it shuts off all the good things it does in your brain and begins to make life miserable for you. This is its way of moving your brain's priority from coping with the stress to ensuring your survival. Don't blame the cortisol. It is only doing what it is designed to do. And as I will say many times throughout this book, feeling good always takes second priority to preserving life.

Also, try training your ears to listen to friends' laughing, water lapping against the shore, and faraway birds. Work at enhancing your touch so holding someone's hand means something or so that you can actually feel the wind. Try to

> Feeling good always takes second priority to preserving life.

notice the good smells of wonderful food. Eat slowly so that your taste buds can come back to life and take the flavors and smells of good food to new heights. It may sound a bit hokey, but these enhanced little pleasures can work wonders in your brain.

STRESS MANAGEMENT FOR DUMMIES

As every reader knows, many health and emotional problems can be traced back to stress. These include depression, chronic pain, chronic fatigue, anxiety, immune deficiencies, and cardiovascular disease, to name but a few. High stress can also be responsible for aggravating autoimmune disorders such as fibromyalgia, chronic fatigue, arthritis, premature menopause, and many more.

But important as these stress-related disorders are, here I want to focus on how modern stress is contributing to the decline in our capacity for pleasure and happiness.

Unlike our ancient forbears, we live in a time when stress is constant, not intermittent. Sure, our ancestors experienced acute demands and periods of extremely high stress, such as floods, epidemics of illness, and droughts. Life on this earth has never been easy. But no matter how severe the stress, it did not last long and was quickly followed by periods of low stress and rest. People slept longer and worked far less than we do, especially before the industrial age.

STRESS AND SOCIAL BREAKDOWNS

Modern-day stress also suffers from what is called social fragmentation. We are lonely people. Twenty-five percent of people do not have a close confidant. Many complain that they don't have time for friendships. Even children are overscheduled and have no connectivity with extended family, such as uncles, aunts, and cousins. Changing jobs or schools disconnects us from friends and forces us to build new friendships, when we don't have the time. And the Beatles's song "All the Lonely People" is about as prophetic as one can get.

Here is a lesson to be learned about modern stress: the stress of earlier times was intermittent, but ours is constant. They had time for recovery built into their lives; we do not. Everyone was connected in some way to a larger support system that helped to ameliorate the effects of stress. The adrenal emergency system is precisely that—an emergency system. If we do not build enough time into our lives to allow recovery of the system, we pay for it in stress disease.

What does this lack of recovery time have to do with anhedonia? Plenty! When stress becomes persistent—as in our modern, driven, and overstimulated lifestyle—our stress hormones change their focus and shift from helping us cope with our stress to protecting us from self-destruction. They make our lives more painful as a way of telling us that we are destroying ourselves.

The many ways our stress hormones operate go beyond the scope of this book, but we all need to know about one such effect: cortisol moves to block many of the brain's emotional neurotransmitters (serotonin and norepinephrine), leading to anhedonia and, if we don't interrupt the process, clinical depression. But cortisol can also block the pleasure neurotransmitter dopamine, which, as you will recall, is the main gratification messenger in the pleasure system. This is why clinical depression always has anhedonia as one of its main symptoms, along with sadness and lethargy. Depressed people cannot enjoy anything and don't have the energy to find something that can give them pleasure.

> If we do not build enough recovery into our lives to allow recovery of the system, we pay for it in stress disease.

HOW MODERN-DAY STRESS HAS CHANGED

Twenty-first-century stress is not the same as twentieth-century stress. Stress today is different from all previous times in two respects.

First, modern-day stress has increased with the accelerated pace of modern life. My grandchildren can hardly tell if they're coming or going, or as we would have said in my day, "They don't know whether they are Arthur or Martha!" Several studies have highlighted how much more children have to learn today—how much kids have to cram into their brains to keep up, let alone succeed. The information highway, while in one sense a blessing, has upped stress for many of us.

Second, our modern technology has reduced the availability of recovery time. Every system in the body needs rest. We have to rest our brain, rest our body, and rest our emotions. Above all, the adrenal system, responsible for sending out stress hormones like adrenaline and cortisol, needs rest also. With enough rest, these systems serve us well. But without adequate recovery time, they fail us because we are pushing them outside their normal limits. Stress disease is the price we pay for this lack of recovery time.

HOW STRESS ROBS YOU OF PLEASURE

I have already made the point that stress robs us of pleasure in the long run. But in what specific ways does stress steal pleasure from ordinary life events?

Stress can interfere with the pathways that carry the message of delight to your pleasure center. I previously mentioned nonsadness depression; the cardinal symptom of this form of depression is anhedonia. In other words, there are many people who may not look depressed but suffer from varying degrees of anhedonia. Their lives are lusterless, unenjoyable, drab, faded, dull, and boring. While once they had a zest for living, now they just go through the motions of their dull, daily lives. And stress can be the major cause of this form of depression.

> Stress can directly overstimulate the pleasure system, thus shutting it down.

Stress can directly overstimulate the pleasure system, thus shutting it down. Adrenaline, our emergency hormone, has one very important function to perform, along with all the other things it does to help us survive the emergency. It also sends a signal to the pleasure system that gives us an enhanced feeling of well-being. In times of crisis, our bodies are designed to cope better with this *feel-good* reaction. It is also called an *adrenaline fix*, a rush of energizing power that makes us feel like we can take on the world.

Excessive use of our adrenal system (for example, in thrill-seeking behaviors) can shut down pathways to the pleasure system. Adrenaline is a stimulant. Following a period of intense activity or stress, like having a daughter get married or completing a project that has captivated you, your adrenal system stops surging. It does so in order to rejuvenate itself. Our adrenal system is designed to help us in times of emergency, not to get us

> If you feel stressed out, depressed, or extremely anhedonic, seek help right away.

through everyday activity. This shutting down of the adrenal system is called *postadrenaline fatigue* because this is precisely what it does—it turns on our fatigue so that we will give it time to recover. We also become irritable and restless. And here is the kicker: it also shuts down our pleasure system to prevent us from running off and enjoying more stressful activity.

EVALUATING YOUR STRESS LEVEL

Before proceeding to the next chapter, let's pause so you can evaluate your stress level.

Just how stressed are you? Since it is nigh impossible for a person to subjectively evaluate his or her own stress (the person often enjoys the stress too much and doesn't realize how harmful it is), here is a test. It has been specifically designed to measure the unique form of stress that impacts your pleasure system. It is not specific to evaluating cardiac disease risk—for such an assessment you need to consult my book on stress, *The Hidden Link Between Adrenaline and Stress*.[3]

STRESS ASSESSMENT SCALE

There are many stress questionnaires out there, but this one is specific to evaluating your risk of stress-induced anhedonia.

Instructions

Use the following scale to enter a score for each question:

0 = Never or rarely

1 = Occasionally (I seem to be able to control it)

2 = Often (several times a week, but for a long time)

3 = Always (every day, and for a lot of the time)

Score

1. I feel pain in the center of my chest that is not due to heart problems. _____

2. My throat feels constricted, and I have difficulty swallowing. _____

3. I have sexual difficulties and have lost sexual desire. _____

4. I am dissatisfied with the work I do and wish I could do something else. _____

5. I feel tired, fatigued, exhausted, or have low energy as if I am run-down. _____

6. I have sleep difficulties or sleep fewer than seven hours a night. _____

7. I explode easily at even inconsequential things. _____

8. I get bored easily and look for activities to cheer me up. _____

9. I need a fix, like buying something or going somewhere, to perk me up. _____

10. My heart feels like it races or skips beats. _____

11. I prefer the excitement of the Internet over
    spending time with friends.   _____

12. I catch a cold or get the flu more often than
    my friends.   _____

13. I get sadder, more anxious, or moodier than
    anyone else I know.   _____

14. I am overcome with shaking or trembling.   _____

15. I am forgetful, disorganized, or lack concentration. _____

Total   _____

Scoring and Interpretation

Total the score given to each question. The highest possible score
is 45.

 0 to 10: Your stress level is very low.

11 to 15: You have mild stress symptoms.

16 to 20: Your stress level is moderate and you may be beginning
          to show some anhedonia.

21 to 25: Your stress level is high, and you may be at risk for
          developing some form of addiction.

26 to 30: Your stress level is very high. Anhedonia may already be
          profound, and you should seek professional help.

Over 31: Your stress level is severe. You may be clinically
         depressed, and you need professional help.

Notwithstanding your score, if you feel stressed out, depressed, or
extremely anhedonic, seek help right away. These are problems that
readily respond to the right treatment.

The topic of stress is not just an adult one, and many of the stress problems facing adults today are much worse in children and teenagers. As I examine the child's stressful world in the next chapter and offer some solutions to the stress in their lives, parallels with adult stress will become evident. So will some of the strategies for lowering stress. So read on.

SAVING OUR CHILDREN
FROM ANHEDONIA

You are worried about seeing your child spend his
early years in doing nothing. What! Is it nothing
to be happy? Nothing to skip, play, and run around
all day long? Never in his life will he be so happy again.
—JEAN-JACQUES ROUSSEAU, *EMILE*

Oh boy, do we have a problem! Our children are in danger, but few really see the real peril. From preschoolers to teenagers, this generation is well on the way to anhedonia, but nobody seems to notice.

The problem of modern-day anhedonia has no more serious a target than our precious children and teenagers. Kids today, aided and abetted by parents, as well as by the media and our culture, are slowly moving toward a pleasureless existence.

Why, only recently while speaking to the faculty of a prestigious Christian college and seminary, I asked several of the professors to identify what characterized modern college students, as compared with students in earlier times. They all gave the same response: students seem incapable of extracting any contentment or pleasure out of the ordinary things of their life. I was totally taken by surprise as I had not even mentioned my interest in modern-day anhedonia. These professors all seemed to know all about the anhedonic new world of young people—a world in which only the spectacular or the extravagant can penetrate the barriers to the pleasure system of young people. Most of the faculty also acknowledged that they were having the same feelings themselves.

> This generation is well on the way to anhedonia, but nobody seems to notice.

TEEN ANHEDONIA ON THE MARCH

For a glimpse into the reasons for this increasing state of child and teen anhedonia, you need look no further than a recent edition of *Time* magazine.[1] The cover article was entitled "Are Kids Too Wired for Their Own Good?" It deals in-depth with the pluses and minuses of children and teens doing everything at once. These kids are aptly being called the *multitasking generation*—or simply Gen M.

The report opens with the story of a Van Nuys family who occupy a three-bedroom home, but psychologically each exists in his or her own little universe. While Mom is tidying up and Dad wolfs down his dinner alone, having missed supper with the kids, the teenage son is at his computer where he is chasing down pictures on Google Images so he can build a shrine to an actress he worships. Several IM windows are also open while he converses with a MySpace pal. Naturally, iTunes is also open, blasting out a deafening mix of several pop musicians. And all this is occurring while the teenager is working on his school homework for the day.

In another room, the teenage daughter is pretty much doing the same thing. "You must multitask," she explains to the reporter, defending her ability to listen to music while doing her homework. She also boasts about being able to talk on her cell phone with the phone's earpiece in one ear and her iPod's earpiece playing music in the other.

WHY PARENTS SHOULD BE CONCERNED

Frightening? Downright alarming, according to researchers interviewed in the article. Worrisome? Apparently not to many parents. They feel relieved that teenagers have something to occupy themselves with these days. Kids these days seem to take multitasking for granted, and many report that it is a good thing. As one parent, a prominent surgeon, said to me just the other day when I made reference to the *Time* article, "I suppose if kids couldn't do more than one thing at a time they wouldn't be able to get anything done at all"— referring, of course, to the tremendous pressure teens are under today.

> Kids these days seem to take multitasking for granted, and many report that it is a good thing.

Well, as we will see, parents ought to be concerned. Right now, thirty-two families in the Los Angeles area are participating in an intensive, four-year study conducted by UCLA on the effects of modern life on the family. While multitasking is not the primary focus of this study, it is showing dramatic change when compared with a study conducted twenty years ago.

While teens feel confident that they can engage in a number of activities at once and still be learning something, many experts doubt it.

For instance, kids are so obsessed with what they are doing that they don't give parents the time of day. So if nothing else, it has devastating effects on the structure of family relationships. School life is also affected. Here are some alarming facts from the *Time* report, important enough for me to mention here:

* A survey of Americans ages eight to eighteen reveals that it is not that kids were spending a larger chunk of time using electronic media—that was holding steady at 6.5 hours a day (could it possibly get any bigger?)—but that they were packing more media exposure into that time: 8.5 hours' worth, listening to iTunes, watching a DVD, and IMing friends all at the same time.

* The phenomenon of multitasking has reached a kind of warp speed in an era of Web-enabled computers.

* Although multitasking kids may be better prepared in some ways, many cognitive scientists are alarmed by the trend. "Kids that are instant messaging while doing homework, playing games online, and watching TV, I predict, aren't going to do well in the long run," says the chief of a cognitive neuroscience laboratory at a major university.

* Many educators and psychologists say parents need to actively ensure that their teenagers break free of compulsive engagement with screens and spend time in the physical company of human beings, because so many kids lead highly scheduled lives that leave little time for old-fashioned socializing and family meals. Indeed, many teenagers and college students say overcommitted schedules drive much of their multitasking.

* It is important for parents and educators to teach kids, preferably by example, to occasionally slow down, unplug, and take time to think about something for a while.

* "The problem," says a Massachusetts psychiatrist, "is what you are not doing if the electronic moment grows too large. You are not having family dinner, you are not having conversations, you are not debating whether to go out with a boy who wants to have sex on the first date, you are not going on a family ski trip or taking time just to veg. It's not so much that the video game is going to rot your brain, it's what you are not doing that's going to rot your life."

* A professor at Stanford University commented that students cannot go the few minutes between classes without talking on a cell phone. It's as if there is an intolerable discomfort among teenagers (and a growing number of adults as well, I might add) when they are not being stimulated—a kind of "I can't stand the silence" feeling that is common in anhedonia.

* A recent study of high school students who used their cell phones more than ninety times a day discovered that the most common reason given was that they were unhappy or bored. (Anhedonia?) They also found that these teens were also significantly more depressed and anxious than their peers who used their phones fewer than seventy times a day.

Concerned social scientists and educators are just beginning to tackle this problem, so we can expect to hear a lot more about this phenomenon in the near future.

PUSHY PARENT SYNDROME

But the problem goes further in that some parents are making it worse. Many parents demand success from their children at any cost. Parents tend to deny this because it has a negative connotation, even when it is true.

According to Dr. Madeline Levine, "Parents who pressure their children to succeed are condemning a generation of middle-class youngsters to stress and depression," and, I would add, to a lifetime of anhedonia.[2] A clinical psychologist, Dr. Levine has identified a variation of the pushy parent—a growing breed of *helicopter* parents, so called because they hover over all aspects of their children's lives. Mostly high earning, they push their children to excel at everything from math to music, science to sports. The result, again, is that these children are overstimulated, and most grow up miserable and confused whenever they fall short of their parents' expectations. At a time in life when they are supposed to be honing their pleasure center to receive joy from many aspects of life, these children end up feeling like helpless and hopeless failures. They learn that they are unhappy and that there is no joy in living. No wonder so many of them commit suicide.

> Many parents demand success from their children at any cost.

It is not surprising, then, that children from affluent homes are three times more likely to be depressed and anxious than the average teenager. They are also at greater risk of resorting to drug abuse (they've got to find some pleasure somewhere), self-harming (feeling pain is better than feeling nothing), and even suicide (what is there to live for?). And it is the struggle to please overambitious parents that lies at the heart of these problems.

So, helicopter parent, ground yourself. You are hampering your children's development, including the neurological growth of a healthy pleasure center, by denying them the joys of normal growing up—taking a walk down to the river with Dad to catch fish, learning to crochet with Mom, or visiting a museum or the zoo—all with a parent, not a class from school where you have some assignment to report.

Children should be given space to explore many interests and not to have their self-esteem challenged by unreasonable demands that cannot be met. Families should eat together, play together, and hike together, and you should create a panoply of family traditions that will reside in their memory and be the source of much pleasure later in life when they recall these happy times together.

TEENAGE MULTITASKING ADDICTION

But my concern goes much further than how learning has been impacted by teenage stress. What was not reported by *Time* magazine is how multitasking sets up the conditions that make it easy for teens to turn to addictive behaviors and substances to find the pleasures they are missing. A high level of multiprocessing and simultaneous multisensory inputting has destructive effects on the pleasure system of the brain—a setup for anhedonia. As the *Time* article reports, the habit of dividing one's attention into many small pieces has significant implications for the way young people learn, reason, socialize, and do creative work. But it also has implications for how and where teenagers get their pleasures.

> A high level of multiprocessing and simultaneous multisensory inputting has destructive effects on the pleasure system of the brain—a setup for anhedonia.

This jumping about in the brain, called *toggling*, is not only ineffective for learning, but many scientists are now saying it also produces significant stress. Yet the stress produced by toggling is not the sort that is unpleasant; it is a good feeling that ups the flow of stress hormones—with consequent damage. Multitasking allows little time for stress recovery.

✳

TEST FOR MULTITASKING ADDICTION

Definition

Multitasking is engaging in the use of multiple activities or sources of stimulation, such as MP3 players, iPods, the Internet, cell phones, or television, at the same time.

(Note: While this test can be taken by a teenager, he or she might downplay the seriousness of the problem. I recommend you work through the test yourself as applied to the teenager(s) in your life.)

Instructions

To assess your teenager's level of addiction to multitasking, use the following scale to enter a score for each question:

0 = Never or rarely

1 = Occasionally (seems to be able to control it)

2 = Often (several times a week, but for a long time)

3 = Always (every day, and for a lot of the time)

Score

1. Your teenager neglects household chores in order to multitask. _____

2. He or she prefers the excitement of being stimulated

by multiple tasks over spending time with friends. _____

3. You have to cajole your teenager to stop a computer activity in order to come to dinner or family activity. _____

4. Your teenager's interaction with friends is mainly via the Internet. _____

5. Multitasking is clearly having a detrimental effect on your teenager's grades. _____

6. Multitasking is clearly having a detrimental effect on your teenager's relationships with friends and family. _____

7. Your teenager loses sleep because he or she spends time multitasking. _____

8. Your teenager appears depressed or moody but cheers up when multitasking. _____

9. When the means for multitasking is not available (computer down, cell phone not working, and so on), your teenager becomes moody or angry. _____

10. Your teenager appears unable to fully enjoy anything that doesn't involve multitasking. _____

Total _____

Scoring and Interpretation

Total the score given to each question. The highest possible score is 30.

0 to 10: Your teenager does not appear to be addicted to multitasking and is able to exercise appropriate control.

11 to 14: Your teenager may be experiencing occasional dependence on multitasking and may be showing signs of a growing addiction.

15 to 17: Your teenager is clearly addicted to multitasking and probably needs some help in regaining control.

18 to 20: Your teenager's use of multitasking is excessive; addiction will become evident and the problem needs to be addressed with some degree of urgency.

Over 20: Indicates a major addiction to multitasking. Seek professional help.

If you are concerned about your teenager's dependence on multitasking, I recommend you seek professional help from a psychologist with expertise in addictions as soon as possible, notwithstanding your teenager's score on this test.

"I JUST GOTTA HAVE IT!"

Conspicuous consumption, according to many experts, dominates the teenage mind; having things is a form of self-expression. What teenagers crave is anything that will announce their identity to the world. From flashy phones to designer jeans, shiny lip gloss to stylish sneakers, they *just gotta have it*.

> Parents have every right to be worried about their children growing up too fast.

Complicating the need to define an identity of their own choosing (this is what kids do on MySpace.com, where they can make up any identity they like—even live out a fantasy identity) is the fact that childhood is ending sooner than ever before. Parents have every right to be worried about their children growing up too fast. It is physiologically true that today's thirteen-year-olds are more mature physically than they were a generation ago.

What is more alarming from the perspective of the focus of this book is that kids today are being immersed in pleasure-intense activities such as sexual overstimulation at an ever decreasing age. Where is it going to stop? No one knows.

"I JUST GOTTA HAVE IT—NOW!"

I recently came across the following blog on the Internet:

> I somehow just can't get over my need for instant gratification, and it is messing up my life. I figure it is not my fault really. I was raised in a world of fast food, and I live in the age of the Internet. Anything in the world is at my fingers at just the touch of a button. Or is it? You see that is the problem. I've been fed all of this hype about how I can do anything or have anything or be anything just by wanting it, and it is all a big fat lie.[3]

This honest revelation says it all. Instant gratification undermines our pleasure system. You may think that getting what we want should build pleasure—after all, our pleasure comes instantly. But the problem with instant gratification is it bypasses normal pleasure-inducing mechanisms, like the joy of anticipating the gift your father has promised you for your birthday. The pleasure is in the waiting, in anticipating something very special that is yet to happen, not the actual receiving. When it comes instantly, the pleasure passes away just as quickly.

DOS AND DON'TS FOR PARENTS OF MULTI-TASKING TEENAGERS

DON'T

- Condemn any behavior you haven't made an effort to understand.
- Expect your child to reduce multitasking when you are overdoing it yourself.
- Give in to your teenager's temper tantrums, pouting, or bad-mouthing.
- Label your teenager as bad or withdraw your love to condemn behavior. Your child is always entitled to your respect and unconditional love.
- Let technology intimidate you. Some parents don't set limits because they are afraid it will show their ignorance.

DO

- Learn how to use the Internet as it increases

I can remember learning this lesson early in my life. Mind you, the definition of *instant* has changed considerably since then. It used to happen at Christmastime. Waiting for Christmas to come was slow and painful for me. But because of my whining one Christmas, my father gave me one of my gifts a week before the magic day. I thought I was in heaven—briefly. Then the pleasure vanished as quickly as it came. You see, much of the real pleasure was in anticipating the Christmas gifts.

The following Christmas, my father offered to give me one of my gifts early again, but I quickly declined and never whined again about how terrible it was to have to wait for a gift you know you're going to get. I had learned my lesson and even today relish waiting to open gifts. Expectation can make pleasure so much more pleasurable. No doubt about it. And impulsiveness robs us of an opportunity to develop a healthier pleasure system.

THE PAIN-PLEASURE CONNECTION

We now turn to an even more serious problem for teenagers. It is growing like a pumpkin on fertilizer steroids.

If you take a close look at any annotated picture of the brain, you will find something quite startling: the pain center of the brain is right next to the pleasure center. Pain and pleasure share an unsettling companionship. Personally, I wish the centers were strangers and existed at the opposite ends of my brain.

Given this proximity, is it possible that the brain cannot sometimes tell the difference between the two? Or, alternatively, does pain sometimes bring us pleasure, whereas pleasure seldom brings us pain? As we will see, these are exceedingly important questions to which we must find some answers if we are to protect our children from a miserable future of unremitting anhedonia.

I picked up our local newspaper

your credibility to set limits.
- Monitor all multitasking activities and limit the number to as few as possible—preferably only one at a time.
- Reinforce behavior that focuses on single activities (praise it, reward it).
- Set clear limits to both time and intensity of all activities that are stimulating.
- Encourage relaxation, taking time out, going outside, changing the environment.
- Foster as much physical activity as you can. This counteracts the high level of stimulation by helping the body burn off excess adrenaline.
- Make sure you set up an Internet monitoring program that limits access to certain undesirable Web sites.

the other morning and sat down for a quick read of the day's news. And there, staring right at me, was a headline supporting my concern: "Resorting to Self-Injury: Students Inflicting Wounds to Express Angst."[4]

This alarming report was not news to me, but it confirmed an epidemic trend that is now disturbing psychologists around the world. The article reported that nearly one in five students at Ivy League schools say they have purposely injured themselves by cutting, burning, or other methods. Counselors report that this type of behavior is happening all across the country as well as in Australia, the United Kingdom, and Europe, at colleges, middle and high schools, and now also in children as young as grade-schoolers.

> If we hurt ourselves repeatedly, as children who cut do, our brains will begin to confuse pain with pleasure.

Fueling this self-injury trend are more than four hundred Web sites devoted to self-inflicted pain, including many that glorify self-injury. They offer graphic photographs and how-to information. The online community on these Web sites help socially isolated kids to feel like they belong.

Why are children and teens turning to self-inflicted pain? That's the million-dollar question. Some kids report (and I have heard this from my own grandchildren who keep me informed about what is going on in their world) that self-injury soothes their anxiety and helps them let other people know they are hurting inside. Their pain reassures them that they are normal—and when you can't feel pleasure in anything else, self-injury is actually quite comforting.

There is no doubt that self-injury creates a rush of endorphins, the brain's natural pain-killing hormones, and so it can easily become an addiction. Ask any long-distance jogger, and he will tell you that an endorphin rush is fantastic. Many of the teens who cut themselves appear to be suffering from clinical depression, which, as we will see in the next section, is now epidemic in our culture. If so, then self-injury is a way for them to get past the anhedonic part of their depression. But it doesn't heal their diminished pleasures.

I believe it goes further than this. Yes, there is profound anhedonia in children and teenagers today, and the experimentation with self-inflicted pain provides a temporary rush of a highly pleasurable painkiller that surges from within the brain. But if we hurt ourselves repeatedly, as children who cut do, our brains will begin to confuse pain with pleasure. After a while, we cannot tell the one from the other.

Shocking? It should be to all of us, because we are beginning to see behavioral problems in more and more of our children based on this pain-pleasure connection. Our kids actually like it when they hurt themselves physically, because it helps to mask the deeper emotional pain they don't want to feel.

CHILDHOOD DEPRESSION—
A COMMON JOY SUCKER

Now we come to the biggest robber of all childhood pleasure. A prominent psychiatrist, Dr. Joan Luby of Washington University School of Medicine in St. Louis, believes the most specific symptom of depressive disorders in kids under age six is something called *anhedonia*— essentially, appearing not to have fun while at play.

Dr. Luby also believes that enjoying activities in play is essential to a child's life, so if you notice that your child consistently doesn't want to play or doesn't seem to enjoy playtime, it is a cold signal that your child may need to be clinically assessed for depression.[5]

Childhood depression has been one of my major areas of research interest for the last twelve years. Children, more so now than in previous times, get depressed. The increase in the incidence of childhood depression is not due just to better diagnostic skills. The stressors that I have described earlier in this chapter are the main cause.

Even preschoolers are now at risk for depression at an unprecedented level. Children this young are incapable of telling a parent they are depressed, and many parents miss the telltale signs of depression. The signs of childhood depression are not the same as in adult depression. Children tend to mask their depression behind such problems as stomachaches, muscle pains, and, of course, anhedonia. Depressed children, no matter how young, lose their capacity to experience pleasure. Sometimes it is the only symptom you can see. Hence my discussion of the topic.

Given how destructive depression can be to children, I want to alert you to the role that anhedonia plays in young children's lives, making our most precious and innocent life partners miserable. So I would like to provide parents and teachers with some help here, not only in enabling them to identify the anhedonia of depression as early as possible but also to offer some solutions to this vexing problem.

HOW TO TELL IF A CHILD IS DEPRESSED

My research has focused on finding a physiological way to diagnose depression in very young children. The early identification of depression is crucial. Depression must be treated as soon as it arrives; otherwise, it becomes entrenched in a child's brain.

In looking for a way to diagnose early childhood depression, I have focused on ways to measure a child's anhedonia. If we can find anhedonia, we will find depression. As in all depression, depressed children lose their capacity for pleasure. So let me describe the technique I use in my laboratory, and it might help you notice a child's depression as well. It's really quite simple.

I have a child watch a series of pictures presented on a large computer screen and measure, with sensitive instruments, changes in their smile and frown reflexes. Normal children smile readily at funny pictures. Depressed children do not smile. So as the child watches the pictures, I measure the changes in the tension of several muscles on the child's face, particularly the muscles that cause the child to smile and frown. I can detect the start of the slightest smile long before you can notice it on the child's face.

> Depression must be treated as soon as it arrives; otherwise, it becomes entrenched in a child's brain.

Before I describe this procedure any further, I want you to sit in front of a mirror and be ready to look up at your face closely as you continue to read. Take a moment to observe yourself smiling. Can you see how the muscles on either side of your mouth form your smile? Now frown, and observe how the muscles on the inner edge of your eyebrows cause the frown. This is where the electrodes are placed and the reactions recorded—for a smile or a frown.

Then we present the pictures to the child, displaying them for five seconds while we record muscle changes. Some of the pictures are neutral in their emotional content (a broom or book), and there is no change in the child's facial expression. Some are negative (like an angry face), so a normal child will frown. Some are happy (smiling babies looking up at you or an ice cream cone), at which a normal child smiles broadly.

A QUICK TEST FOR CHILDHOOD DEPRESSION

Now for the quick test you can use. I am going to describe one of the pictures, one that creates a huge smile in normal children but tends to get more of a frown in depressed children. As soon as I have described the picture, look at your face in the mirror.

Ready? Here's the picture: imagine an adorable puppy, head cocked to one side with a quizzical look, wearing a long, colorful tie. What do you see in the mirror? If you are normal, you should see a big smile. If you were connected to my instruments, I would be measuring a very large muscle change in your smile muscles. Of course, we don't rely on just one picture. There are at least ten happy pictures in the set of thirty that elicit a smile from normal children. When a child doesn't smile at most of them, you have depression. Remember, depressed children suffer from the same deficiency as depressed adults—they cannot enjoy anything.

So how can a parent or teacher recognize the beginnings of anhedonia before it becomes a full-blown depression? Well, think about the puppy with the tie. There are many such happiness-producing stimuli in a child's life. By paying attention to how your child responds, say, to a funny movie where other children are laughing while your child is not, you need to consider the possibility of a milder form of anhedonia. Or to use another example, let's say you give a child a gift and do not get any happy response; you need to consider whether anhedonia is present. This may point to the possibility of the child being clinically depressed, or it may be that the child is being overstimulated and thus reducing his or her capacity for normal pleasure. If so, then you need to explore for your child the principles offered in the second part of this book.

To help a parent or teacher evaluate a child's level of anhedonia, I have also prepared the following test:

❊

TEST FOR CHILDHOOD ANHEDONIA

The person making this evaluation needs to be someone who is close to the child such as a live-in parent or guardian. Also, this evaluation will not be valid if disorders like childhood autism, schizophrenia, or brain damage are present.

Instructions

Use the following scale to enter a score for each question:

0 = Rarely, or doesn't apply

1 = Occasionally (several times a month)

2 = Often (several times a week)

3 = Always

Score

1. Your child does not enjoy candy, ice cream, or other delights. _____

2. Your child seems to be numb and cannot respond to happy events. _____

3. Your child seems to have a sad expression. _____

4. Other children seem to be much happier than your child. _____

5. The worst time of the day for your child is the morning or after a nap. _____

6. Your child is grouchy or irritable, and easily loses his or her temper. _____

7. You cannot think of anything that can make your child happy. _____

8. Your child does not like to give or receive affection. _____

9. Your child complains about stomachache. _____

10. Your child does not want to socialize or play with playmates. _____

Total _____

Scoring and Interpretation

Total the score given to each question. The highest possible score is 30.

0 to 6: Your child appears to have normal pleasure response.

7 to 12: There might be mild anhedonia in some areas of your child's life.

13 to 18: Your child is beginning to show moderate anhedonia.

19 to 24: You child has significant anhedonia. If it continues, he or she may need some help.

25 to 30: Your child's anhedonia is serious and needs professional help. Clinical depression needs to be ruled out.

Since severe anhedonia can indicate that a child is clinically depressed, an important question arises—namely, how can a parent tell if depression, rather than an overstimulated or hijacked pleasure center, is responsible? I have tried to exclude depression-specific symptoms from the above test, but, unfortunately, there is a lot of overlap.

Depression is indicated if the following symptoms are also present in your child:

* Sleep disturbances such as insomnia, excessive sleepiness, or early morning waking

* Suicidal ideation or death wishes ("I wish I was dead")

* Cries easily

* Impaired school performance

* Picking fights with other children

Obviously, if your child is displaying clear signs of depression, you should seek professional help right away. Many parents are reluctant to do this because they feel they might be responsible for their child's depression. Let me hasten to assure you, depression strikes the best of families—as I know very well. It is not a sign of bad or neglectful parenting, and even if you could do your parenting all over again, the outcome would probably be the same.

Parents these days have to contend with a world that puts children at risk for many stress disorders, including depression. Your responsibility is to seek the proper treatment as soon as possible. If you fear failing as a parent, neglecting to take timely action is a legitimate reason to fear failing. Treatment for depression in children includes psychotherapy in an individual, group, or family format. Medication may also be indicated. (For more information on teenage depression, see the book I wrote together with my daughter Dr. Catherine Hart Weber—*Stressed or Depressed*.)[6]

HELP FOR STRESSED-OUT PARENTS

Let me close this chapter with some soothing medicine for stressed-out parents and overscheduled kids. The advice comes from the American

Academy of Pediatrics, no less, and says that this is what modern children need—more free time. Good, old-fashioned playtime.[7]

Parents have become convinced that they have to give their children more scheduled time, get-smart videos, enrichment activities, and lots of classes to help them excel. Such pressure often begins in infancy. What is being sacrificed, the academy says, is spontaneous free play—chasing butterflies, playing with toys like dolls and blocks, or just plain romping on the floor with mom and dad.

> Stop trying to be a superparent. Put on your jeans and sneakers and go outside and play with your kids a little.

And herein lies several keys to starting early in preventing your children, even as young as preschoolers, from becoming anhedonic:

* Above all else, give a high priority to making time for your children. Get involved in their interests—play with their hamsters or dolls. This fosters a healthy pleasure system.

* Do not push too much excitement or stimulation on your children. Instead, let them set the pace and don't have unreasonable expectations for them.

* Build in recovery and relaxation time when you engage, as a family, in low-key activities such as sitting together and talking or taking walks.

The American Academy of Pediatrics cites numerous studies to support their contention that pushing children beyond their abilities, a *get smart at any cost* strategy, fosters obesity, depression, and high stress—and, I might also add, an inability to extract pleasure from the simple things of life. Furthermore, children who are overscheduled with structured activities are missing the chance they have to dream, to fantasize, to make their own world work the way they want it. That's what a lot of experts are now telling us, and I have not heard truer words of wisdom for childrearing in a long time.

So stop trying to be a superparent. Put on your jeans and sneakers and go outside and play with your kids a little. You might find it lowers your stress as well. And if you don't have the time to do it, at least reduce the number of activities for them and tell your kids to go play. I can guarantee that one day your kids will look back on these fun times and say, "That was the happiest time of my life."

WHEN PLEASURE BECOMES
A HIDDEN ADDICTION

No pleasure is a bad thing in itself, but the things
which produce pleasures entail disturbances
many times greater than the pleasures themselves.
—EPICURUS

The pursuit of pleasure is not without its dark side. While it is essential that the brain's pleasure system is kept in tip-top condition, we literally walk a tightrope here. Stay on the rope, and you will travel toward a rich and fulfilling life. Miss your step by pursuing pleasure too eagerly and greedily, and you can fall into the depths of despair.

The greatest menace associated with greedy pleasure is that it can become a hidden addiction (addictions that are based not on substances but on behavior such as pornography or gambling). Or worse still, it can spawn a whole cadre of addictions, both substance and hidden. Hidden addictions—involving behaviors such as workaholism, thrill seeking, and Internet games—is the focus of this chapter.

GOOD PLEASURES CAN PRODUCE
BAD CONSEQUENCES

There are many good things in life that can bring us healthy pleasure: affection, food, sex, and music, to name just a few. However, all these pleasures share a common pathway to the brain's pleasure center and have the potential to become addicting. A rather scary connection.

> Everything that gives us pleasure has the potential to become addicting when abused.

Just how powerful these reward pathways are in governing our behavior is most apparent when they are hijacked by addictions to substances or behaviors. As one former cocaine addict confessed:

Everything is about getting high, and any means necessary to get there becomes rational. If it means stealing something from somebody close to you, then you'll do that. If it means lying to your family, borrowing money from people you know you can't pay back, writing checks you can't cover, you do all of those things. It's hard to understand how you continuously spend money and do things that are totally against everything you have ever believed in and get nothing out of it.

It is now indisputable that everything that gives us pleasure has the potential to become addicting when abused. Food, sports, sex, and many other things that are otherwise normal can become addictions. Furthermore, in some people the chemical pathways to the pleasure center may become interrupted by other internal factors, making pleasure harder for them to experience than normal people. For instance, research has shown that people with certain genetic predispositions may be at higher risk for chemical dependency. They may be more impulsive or lack certain enzymes that are needed to remove certain substances. Also, suffering from certain emotional disorders may predispose some people to use addicting substances to medicate their chemical imbalance. So we literally negotiate a minefield here.

HOW HIDDEN ADDICTIONS MIMIC DRUG ADDICTIONS

The process of recovery from a hidden addiction is very similar to recovery from substance addictions. So a few comments on how they mimic each other might be helpful. Research on addiction to cocaine (a powerful stimulant of our pleasure system) has been very helpful here and has taught us a lot about how the brain's pleasure system works—in both substance and behavior addictions.

Everyone knows that cocaine is highly addicting. About 16 percent of those who "just try it once" become instantly hooked on it, so it is not a drug you have to keep taking to become addicted. Cocaine literally rewires the brain more powerfully and quickly than most other addicting drugs. It intensely stimulates the brain's pleasure centers, pro-

> The process of recovery from a hidden addiction is very similar to recovery from substance addictions.

ducing not just a buzz like some drugs but outright euphoria. This is one of the reasons that cocaine can cause such a debilitating addiction.

But it is not only substances that can do this. Many behaviors can do the same. The power of Internet gaming addiction was highlighted recently by a story of several men in Korea who became so addicted to playing Internet video games that they could not stop, even for food, and two cases have been reported of young men dropping dead after seven days of continuous gaming. Internet gambling is equally addicting.

Behavior addictions can also rewire the brain and take the pleasure system hostage to the addicting behavior. Ask people who are addicted to shopping, eating, or risk-taking behavior, and they will tell you that this is the only way they know how to feel good. Take work addiction as an example. While I don't believe that hard work is an addiction, there is clearly a line you cross when you become a true workaholic.

INDUSTRIOUSNESS VERSUS WORK ADDICTION

A very common hidden addiction today is workaholism. Workplace productivity and learned industriousness are currently major points of interest in business and industry, and any attempt to reduce productivity is often met with strong resistance in many quarters. Furthermore, the idea of industriousness is now being touted in work circles. But when does hard work become an addiction? And how is being a hard worker different from workaholism?

Research suggests we can learn to be hard, persistent workers. No surprise here. But the concept does raise certain concerns. Those of us who have been given the right rewards (stimuli for the brain's reward center), often starting in childhood, tend to develop a strong work ethic. We work hard because it feels good. But unless learning to work hard also helps us learn to set clear boundaries to our work and to develop equally important rewards for recreational and self-care activities, we are merely being conned into working habits that profit the workplace but ultimately destroy our personal lives.

This is already the case in Japan where something called *karoshi* is advocated. It literally means *dying from overwork*. Your widow gets a small pension and a certificate to hang on the wall if you drop dead after working a certain number of hours continuously. You will have a tough time trying to convince me that this is a good thing. A healthy work habit must provide a proper balance between working and resting, or else it has the potential to become addicting.

I am a hard worker and can be as productive as anyone. But it is only during the last twenty-five years of my life that I have learned to play as well. Remember the old adage "All work and no play makes Jack a dull boy"? Well, it's not just that you become a *dull* boy. You become a *dead* boy—and sooner than your time. Fortunately, some parts of the industrial and business world are finally getting the message: play is crucial to attaining a work-life balance and ultimately improves productivity as well.

> A healthy work habit must provide a proper balance between working and resting, or else it has the potential to become addicting.

A work-life balance is now the number one concern of employees at all levels in Canada and the U.S. According to recent studies, the ability to achieve this balance is now the top determinant of whether workers are happy on the job and whether they stay or leave.[1] Or, to put it in my simple language, when managers stop messing around with employees' pleasure and reward centers, they will discover that workers actually work harder and accomplish more. Happiness on the job makes us better workers—but in a healthy sense.

So when does overwork become an addiction? A work enthusiast is someone who knows how to work hard but also knows where the boundaries are and can quit. A work addict doesn't. Where is the boundary? You cross it the moment you do any of the following:

* You ignore rest or leisure time in your life.

* Your work interferes with your personal life.

* Your work is destructive to your family's life.

* Your work imprisons you to the extent that you are a slave to your work.

* Your work is the only source of pleasure in your life.

MISUSING OUR PLEASURE BOOSTERS

Behind all the factors that can create hidden addictions lies the overuse of our pleasure system through what I call *pleasure boosters*—extraordinarily stimulating activities that amplify the strength of the pleasure experience. When we cannot feel any pleasure, we develop our own quirky way of boosting our pleasure system, pushing it into high gear. I know I do. That's why I'm writing this book.

So what are some of your pleasure boosters? Here are some of the ways people try to jump-start their pleasure system. They use these activities whenever they feel bored, apathetic, lethargic, or pleasureless:

* Visiting the local shopping mall to see what catches your fancy. Just window-shopping helps boost some people's dull life.

* Buying yourself a gift or gadget that you don't really need or can't really afford is a *magic bullet* that can jump-start a turned-

off pleasure system. It gives you a short-term jolt of pleasure—
and I mean short-term.

* Going to an exciting game (basketball, baseball, football or, in
  the part of the world I come from, rugby or cricket) for the
  express purpose of overcoming your moody state of mind.

* Surfing the Internet with no real objective in mind—just to find
  something to thrill you.

* Bidding on eBay (an online auction house) for something you
  really don't need. Auction buying has an interesting intrigue.
  I believe it is addicting in the same way that gambling is. You
  win some and lose some, and the adrenaline high it gives you
  pays off.

Now add your own pleasure boosters (and be honest about it):

_____

_____

_____

With a little reflection, you could probably come up with a long list
of your own choice pleasure boosters.

ARE PLEASURE BOOSTERS EVER JUSTIFIED?

An important question that many of you are asking is, "Isn't it sometimes justified to turn to some booster to give your pleasure system a
lift? Life can be dull and tedious at times, and a distraction that gives
me a different kind of pleasure feels so good."

The simple answer is yes. We all need activities in our lives that can help to boost our spirits or to get us out of the doldrums. Life would not be worth living if we couldn't find something that can relieve our temporary anhedonia, especially if it is not of our own making. Times of disappointment inevitably arise, and while some sadness is helpful to the grieving process, we must be careful not to settle into a chronic sad state. There comes a time when you have to rise up out of the ashes of your misery, and a pleasure booster might just be what the doctor ordered.

But at the same time we need to heed the dangers of relying too much on these boosters of joy. Persistently boosting your pleasure to overcome your anhedonia carries certain risks.

> Using pleasure boosters to mask or avoid your deeper emotional conflicts is the surest setup for some sort of addiction.

What are these risks? For starters, it can be an expensive solution to a simple problem. I have a friend who has been overstressed and overextended for some time. So what did he do? He saw an advertisement for a Harley Davidson motorcycle that had excitement written all over it. While his family really needed a new car, his craving for some excitement overcame his better sense, and he splurged and bought the motorcycle. Did it fix his problem? Briefly. But the last I saw of it, hidden behind some boxes in his garage, it was collecting dust like a neglected Egyptian mummy.

Another risk is that the pursuit of temporary pleasure through a boost can mask deeper issues you are not facing up to. Perhaps you are not being a good husband, and your wife is extremely unhappy because of the way you are neglecting her. How does jumping on your new motorcycle and vanishing for several hours (a common pleasure booster for many men) solve your deeper problems? In all addictions, the addict is trying to run away from reality. You may feel a brief temporary pleasure, but sooner or later you have to come back down to earth and face your neglected responsibilities.

Using pleasure boosters to mask or avoid your deeper emotional conflicts is the surest setup for some sort of addiction. And lest you quickly try to reassure yourself that you are not a candidate for any major drug addiction, let me remind you that anhedonia can set us all up for so-called hidden addictions—behaviors that make up the more common addictions of respectable people.

INTERNET-DRIVEN PLEASURES

One of the greatest pleasure boosters to come our way in recent times is the Internet. Part of me thinks it is a marvelous invention. I was building computers before they became personal computers and could program them before others even knew what a computer program was. Also, I'm old enough to remember how dull and boring life seemed to be without computers.

So I am very thankful that computer technology appeared during my time on earth. I would have hated being born a century ago. I only hope there are computers in heaven.

However, despite my affinity for computers, it is an indisputable fact that the Internet is a mixed blessing. Through it we have all become tech junkies. Almost every gadget we use, watch, or listen to these days has a computer inside it. Small, yes, but a computer nevertheless.

Calling computers a mixed blessing brings to mind a recent event. I was teaching a graduate class in our doctoral program. The students, all future psychologists, are encouraged to bring laptops to class. Their desks allow them to access the Internet to retrieve information. While lecturing, I noticed several students intensely engaged with their computers. I had occasion to go to the back of the class, but when walking back to the podium, I discovered that they were playing games over the Internet. Definitely a mixed blessing.

STIMULATING GADGETS ARE NOW OUR MAJOR PLEASURE BOOSTERS

Not only are personal computers responsible for a lot of pleasure boosting, but a host of other gadgets are enjoyment jabbers as well. The latest wave includes MP3 players, high-definition television, all-in-one cell phones, and digital video recorders like TiVo—the list goes on and on. All are now considered essential living tools by the average person. And now we have the iPhone, recently released by Apple. This remarkable gadget promises to out-wow anything before. The iPhone combines three products—a revolutionary mobile phone, a widescreen iPod, and a breakthrough Internet communications device with desktop-class e-mail, Web browsing, maps, and searching—in one small and lightweight handheld device. A gadget lover's dream. The iPhone lets you control everything in your world with just the touch of your fingers. The makers claim that it ushers in an era of software power and sophistication never before seen in a mobile device, completely redefining what you can do while you are on the go and, I might add, robbing you further of downtime and raising the threat of even greater overstimulation of the user's pleasure system. I'm tempted to call it *iAnhedonia*!

OK, so I admit that I find gadgets like iPhones and TiVo a fantastic addition to my hungry high-tech world. TiVo allows me to save TV programs so I can watch them at my convenience and without commercials. British comedy and *Masterpiece Theater* are the mainstays of my pleasure boosters, but I consider these to be more relaxing than stimulating. I haven't yet figured out how I will really benefit from an iPhone, but give me a few months.

So are all these gadgets good for us? A little. Unfortunately, they bring in their wake a lot of bad news as well, as CNN recently reported: "Millions of Americans are now showing early signs of addiction to the next wave of high-tech toys, according to an AP poll. And children are leading the way in this newfound form of addiction."[2]

Yes, you read correctly. The CNN report is right on target. All these good things bring a new generation of challenges. How on earth do we keep our pleasure system within the bounds of a healthy, normal response when it is being bombarded with multiple pleasure boosters? How do we prevent our brains from going down the addictions road—a road that leads to misery for those who get hooked?

When used in moderation, these modern advances can help many improve the quality of their lives. Take Jennifer, for instance. She's a typical stay-at-home mother of two young children. "The Internet is my lifeline," she says. "E-mail is my connection to friends when I am hungry for adult conversation or want to share my feelings or get the latest gossip around the neighborhood." She's not alone. I know scores of stay-home-moms who need adult conversations, an escape from screaming kids, and sometimes just some healthy distraction.

So I don't want to sound like a killjoy here, and I readily admit that many high-tech gadgets can help life move along more smoothly for some people. However, there are dangers here that would be foolish for us to ignore. And keep in mind the thesis of this book: the abuse of our pleasure center is creating the pervasive anhedonia that drives our need for excessive excitement and stimulation. In this sense, therefore, the Internet can be a significant cause and a consequence of modern-day anhedonia if misused.

EVALUATING YOUR INTERNET ADDICTION

How can you know if you are already addicted or rapidly tumbling toward being enslaved by your computer? Experts tell us that it isn't simply a matter of how much time you spend online that determines whether you are an addict. Some people can be addicted and may only spend twenty hours a week using the Internet, while others spending forty hours may have no measurable level of addiction.

To a large extent it depends on how much damage the Internet is causing your physical, social, and mental health. Most important—given the focus of this book—is whether it is damaging to your pleasure center. Is your activity on the Internet making it difficult for you to derive pleasure out of other aspects of your life?

Anhedonia caused by Internet addiction is now very common. The high level of stimulation that the multiple, simultaneous tasks a computer offers can seriously flood your dopamine system and rob you of pleasure from the other, more important things in your life. I know—because this is definitely a weak spot in my own life. So when the Internet interferes with your family, relationships, work, school, or just the simple pleasures of life, it is an addiction and the price you are paying is just too high.

> Anhedonia caused by Internet addiction is now very common.

The following test will help you to assess your level of Internet addiction:

TEST FOR INTERNET ADDICTION

Instructions

Use the following scale to enter a score for each question:

0 = Never or rarely

1 = Occasionally (I seem to be able to control it)

2 = Often (several times a week, but for a long time)

3 = Always (every day, and for a lot of the time)

Score

1. You use and stay on the Internet longer than you intend when you sit down in front of your computer. _____

2. Your school grades or your work suffers from how much time you spend on the Internet. _____

3. Your parents or your spouse or friends complain that you spend too much time on the Internet. _____

4. You neglect or forget your chores or other duties because you are spending time on the Internet. _____

5. You become defensive whenever anyone asks you what you are doing on the Internet. _____

6. Your sleep is affected by your being on the Internet (because it robs you of sleep or you cannot get to sleep). _____

7. During the day, you spend time thinking about or anticipating when you will be able to get on the Internet. _____

8. You get mad when someone bothers you when you are on the Internet. _____

9. When your computer or the Internet is down, you get angry or upset to the point where others can see it. _____

10. You tend to check your e-mail compulsively—more
    frequently than is really necessary. _____

11. You prefer the excitement of the Internet to the
    intimacy you can enjoy with your partner, spouse,
    or friends. _____

12. You find that while you say to yourself, I'll stop now,
    you continue working on the computer. _____

13. When you are sad, down, anxious, or moody,
    going on the Internet lifts your mood. _____

14. If you had to choose between the Internet and
    any other social activity, you would choose the
    Internet. _____

15. You have more friends or contacts on the Internet
    than you do in real life. _____

Total _____

Scoring and Interpretation

Total the score given to each question. The highest possible score
is 45.

0 to 10: You probably do not have an Internet addiction.

11 to 20: You have the beginnings of addiction and may be more
    hooked than you realize.

21 to 30: You are an Internet addict, and your addiction may be
    harming your social and personal life.

Over 30: Your Internet addiction is so severe that you should
    consider getting professional help for it.

BREAKING YOUR INTERNET ADDICTION

So what can you do if you are an Internet addict? As with all addictions, you literally have to recover your hijacked pleasure center and find ways to get pleasure from other, more important areas of your life once again.

As in substance addictions, you can go cold turkey (instantly shut it out of your life until you can control it), or you can go slow-poke turkey (gradually wean yourself from it, a little bit each day). Frankly, I believe cold turkey is the best way to deal with Internet addiction. Here's how you can do it:

* Find someone who can serve as an accountability partner for you.

* Discuss just how little Internet activity is really necessary.

* Establish some clear boundaries on what you can and cannot access, as well as the time limits that are reasonable.

* Stick to your boundaries. No excuses!

It doesn't take years of psychotherapy for you to discover what you need to do. You are not the victim of some bad experiences in your earlier life. Just accept that to experience a life that is full of real joy and deep satisfaction, you must retrieve your pleasure center and stop whatever is getting in the way. I've been a psychologist too long to believe that any other way is better.

The second half of this book is devoted to exploring important ancillary steps that must be taken in order to restore a healthy pleasure environment.

POSITIVE ADDICTIONS CAN CREATE
A HEALTHY PLEASURE SYSTEM

There is one additional bit of help I can offer you for recovering from an Internet addiction, or from any addiction for that matter. It is for you to develop some positive addictions in your life—positive habits that can offset the appeal of your negative addictions. Let me explain.

The term *addiction* is usually associated with damaging behaviors or substances, such as drugs, alcohol, food, or smoking. These are powerful forces that can destroy our ability to experience true, healthy pleasure. And they also sap your strength and zest for making the most out of your life.

But are all addictions bad for you? Dr. William Glasser believes there are addicting activities that are strengths, not weaknesses or handicaps. And these positive addictions—repeating habits that may even be a bit compulsive—can actually help to offset the destructive ones. I heartily endorse this idea. Examples of positive addictions include jogging, biking, swimming, meditating, journaling, exercising regularly, relaxing often, and so on.[3]

> Your positive addictions will contribute enormously to your development of a healthy pleasure system.

Dr. Gerald May, in his excellent book called *Addiction and Grace*, agrees with this and has provided some excellent guidelines as to where positive addictions end and destructive ones begin.[4] However, I would add that "it makes me feel good" is not a good enough reason to develop a repetitive habit. All addictions make you feel good. But positive addictions clearly help to serve as a healthy form of pleasure booster, and can, in my opinion, help to restore an anhedonic system.

It takes six months or longer of repetitive positive activity, up to one hour every day, to develop a strength-giving addiction. But I can assure you the time investment is well worth the effort. It can bring significant healing to an otherwise decrepit pleasure system—and some happiness to boot.

Here are some guidelines for developing healthy, positive habits:

1. You must be able to do the activity alone. (This removes any sense of shame or guilt over how good or bad you are at the activity.)
2. The activity must not be competitive. (Competition creates frustration, driving more adrenaline involvement that can be addicting.)
3. You must know when to quit the behavior. (A sure sign of negative addiction is the loss of control over the behavior.)
4. The activity must add some value to your life. (Throwing stones at tin cans can hardly be considered as adding value to your life.)
5. The activity must make no demands or create a striving for excellence; neither must it allow for any self-criticism.
6. In time, you slowly get better at it. (Needing to get better quickly only leads to frustration if you are a slow learner.)

Positive addictions provide enormous benefits—physically, emotionally, and spiritually. I strongly recommend that you take up a positive addiction, follow these six guidelines, and make the activity a regular part of your life. Together with what I recommend in the second part of this book, your positive addictions will contribute enormously to your development of a healthy pleasure system.

SEXUAL ANHEDONIA

How do I love thee?
Let me count the ways.
I love thee to the depth and breadth and height
My soul can reach, when falling out of sight.
—ELIZABETH BARRETT BROWNING

O f all the pleasures the brain is capable of delivering, sensual pleasure, including the ability to love and build intimacy, must surely
be its crown. But there is one important proviso: don't expect to experience the true ecstasy of your sexuality if you separate sensuality from
love and intimacy. They are designed to go together.

The pleasure of sex is not derived purely from physical or hormonal
factors—at least not in its purest and most beautiful form. As history, art,
literature, poetry, and music will attest, sensual pleasure is a beautiful
thing that stands apart from all other pleasures. Why? Because it involves
the whole brain, not just the specific center dedicated to pleasure. And

this is probably the most important bit of information I can offer here: the primary sex organ of the body is not the gonads but the brain.

In this respect, human sexual pleasure bears little resemblance to animal pleasure. As mentioned earlier, humans, like all animals, have a similar center for processing pleasure, but there is one major difference: the activating mechanism in humans is far more complex and the sexual pleasure humans experience is more profound. It is the brain—all of it—that provides this delight. And the emotional relationship of millions of couples suffers whenever sexual pleasure is diminished.

> The primary sex organ of the body is not the gonads but the brain.

The topic of sex and sexual gratification is a large one, so my focus in this chapter will be somewhat narrow. I want to explore how sexual pleasure can be reduced by the hectic overstimulation of both the sexual and pleasure systems in our brains, creating a state of sexual anhedonia (the reduced capacity to experience sexual pleasure in normal human relationships). And nothing can more readily create a state of sexual anhedonia than a sexual addiction, including the persistent use of pornography.

Obviously, if you cannot get any pleasurable response from your brain, you are not likely to foster sexual desire. In this sense, then, sexual anhedonia can result in reduced sexual desire.

SEXUAL ANHEDONIA VERSUS LOW SEXUAL DESIRE

It is important that we understand the difference between sexual anhedonia and lowered sexual desire, so allow me to clarify the distinction. Sexual anhedonia is the reduced capacity of the brain to deliver pleasurable feelings related to sex, while low sexual desire is the lack of any desire to engage your sexual pleasure system in the first place.

Low sexual desire can be present from the start in a marriage and has many causes. One of them could be a generalized anhedonia, such as we commonly see in depression. As I have already suggested, without a normal pleasure system you are not likely to be capable of experiencing sexual pleasure. All pleasure is reduced in general anhedonia, including sexual pleasure.

> All pleasure is reduced in general anhedonia, including sexual pleasure.

In sexual anhedonia, your desire for sex may be normal, even high. But when you engage in sexual activity, it doesn't feel as pleasurable as it did previously—say, as when you first married. It is mainly caused by abuse or excessive use of your sexual system. It feels like something has changed. And it is this *something* that we will explore in this chapter.

STRESS AND SEXUAL ANHEDONIA

As with the other areas I have explored, excessive and chronic stress not only undermines access to our pleasure center, causing a generalized anhedonia, but it also diminishes the experience of sexual pleasure and brings with it a lowered sexual desire.

To illustrate how excessive stress can lead to sexual anhedonia, let me share a story.

I'll call him Brandon. Now in his midforties, Brandon, a devoted Christian, is a dutiful husband and father who for the past two years has been trying to get a business of his own up and running. Having shaped a successful career in sales earlier in his life, he branched out on his own because he felt he could take his business to higher ground if he controlled it. But it has been a challenging two years. First, a global decline in the products he sells made promotion more of a challenge than before. Second, because he was owner of the company, his stress was much higher than it would have been had he worked for someone else.

But Brandon is not a loser. He upped his work hours, set aside all other distractions, even reducing his church-related activities, and gave his business venture all he had to give.

At first, he seemed to thrive on the challenge. It enthused him. No doubt the adrenaline in his body was flowing thick and strong, and every little success he achieved created a bit of euphoria. And even though that feeling was short-lived, it kept him going.

But soon his wife noticed a shift in his recreational priorities. A sports fan, Brandon usually designated certain games he would never miss. It was not a selfish focus on a particular sports event, as he would include his family by making it a family night. And his wife loved the times they could enjoy together. But with the increasing stress, Brandon began forfeiting his game night, insisting that he couldn't get his mind off work, and instead stayed up late planning and strategizing. Succeeding became an obsession.

Then Brandon's wife noticed he had a diminishing interest in sex. At first this didn't faze her, as she found his reduced demands and less frequent need for sex allowed her to enjoy their sex more. But one day she sat up with quite a start. Some months had gone by, and Brandon had expressed no interest in sex. And when she approached him, he declined the offer. His excuse was not the proverbial "I have a headache," but "I've got so much on my plate that I know I won't enjoy it." Welcome to sexual anhedonia. *It's time for some marital therapy,* she wisely thought.

I'll finish this story later.

DEAD-END TO DESIRE

Before I go any further in exploring sexual anhedonia, I need to expand a little on the problem of low sexual desire to show how it differs from sexual anhedonia.

Low sexual desire can be caused by many factors. Often it has a medical cause, such as an illness or hormonal deficiency. It can occur with aging and often after childbirth. When the underlying cause is removed, a robust sexual response may emerge. If the pleasure system is healthy, then why wouldn't it? In sexual anhedonia, however, medical factors are *not* the problem. It is your pleasure center that is the problem. It has been robbed of any pleaure-giving ability.

> In sexual anhedonia, however, medical factors are not the problem. It is your pleasure center that is the problem.

Low sexual desire can be very distressing, especially if it is upsetting an otherwise happy marriage or doesn't seem to have a clearly identifiable cause. Generally, low sexual desire is more common in women than men—but that could be changing. More and more men, especially those who have gotten caught up in some sort of sexual addiction, are finding that they have lost desire for normal sex and can be aroused only by the extraordinary experience their addiction provides. In these cases, it is the wife who has to settle for a sexless marriage, and this can be as distressing for them as it is for men whose wives have low sexual desire.

How common is low sexual desire? Because there is a lot of stigma attached to sexual problems, research here is not always reliable. However, according to the Sex in America study of a decade ago, one in three women and one in seven men reported inhibited sexual desire. Sixteen percent of couples reported a "low-sex relationship."[1] I am sure that the numbers are higher now, but no recent large-scale study that I am aware of has been undertaken to update these statistics. My estimate is that about one in five marriages are now low-sex or no-sex marriages. Not a pretty picture.

Undoubtedly, diminished sexual desire on either partner's part is distressing for couples and is one of the primary reasons for marital distress. But it is not just a problem that develops later in life when aging slowly reduces desire or when couples lose the novelty of their relationship, and it becomes stale. Desire problems plague young couples as much as older ones. It is a myth to think that boredom, age, or familiarity are the main reasons for inhibited sexual desire. No, there are many low-sex, and even no-sex, marriages in younger and newly married couples as well. I have seen many such cases in therapy.

> My estimate is that about one in five marriages are now low-sex or no-sex marriages.

In addition to the problem of sexual anhedonia (a cause often overlooked by sex therapists, marriage counselors, psychologists, and gynecologists), there are many other causes for low sexual desire as well. Here are a few:

For women:
* Painful intercourse
* Sexual abuse in early life
* Sexual phobia (similar to other phobias)
* Ignorance in sexual technique by both partners
* Unrealistic romantic needs (fostered by novels and movies)

* Unsatisfactory parental sexual instruction that created a morbid fear of sex
* Lack of romantic involvement by the husband
* Unreasonable demands for sex (frequency or unusual forms of sex)
* Side effects of some antidepressants or other medications
* Recent childbirth
* Exhaustion

For men:
* Embarrassment over ejaculation problems (too fast or too slow)
* Feelings of inferiority about the size of their penis
* Constant criticism by partner
* Excessive work disappointment or stress
* Low testosterone level
* Unconventional sexual needs fostered by pornography
* Side effects of some antidepressants or other medications
* Midlife or other crisis

Since these problems can seriously threaten a marital relationship, couples should seek appropriate psychotherapy or sex therapy as soon as possible as they arise.

THE CHARACTERISTICS OF SEXUAL ANHEDONIA

Low sexual desire based on sexual anhedonia, as opposed to illness, fear of intercourse, or pain, is clearly a different problem. All of us, even those with an extraordinarily high sex drive, will experience a reduction in our sexual desire from time to time. It can happen when you or your spouse are preoccupied with some major life challenge. Anything that disrupts the normal flow of life can switch off our sexual desire. It can be sudden in onset, and you get over it fairly quickly—or it can be insidious over several years and you hardly notice it. One day you suddenly realize that all your sexual desire has vanished.

You will recall the story I told about Brandon earlier in this chapter. Well, as I began to explore his problem with him, it became clear that this was no ordinary, nature-driven, diminished sexual desire.

> Anything that disrupts the normal flow of life can switch off our sexual desire.

Nor was it an uncommon one. I have seen it many times in patients, especially in recent times. It is becoming more and more common—and not just because men are more open to getting help for reduced sexual desire. It is because of the higher level of stress that comes from our modern-day accelerated pace of life.

Brandon and his wife reported that earlier in their marriage they had been very active sexually. Even after the birth of their second child, when it would be normal for sexual desire to be substantially reduced in the mother, she had continued with an energetic sensuality, and this had helped them to build a very close emotional bond. But now it was different. And Brandon's decreased sexual desire had started shortly after he had thrown all his energies into starting his new business venture.

Brandon was able to describe the change very clearly. No longer did sex provide any pleasure. Pleasure now came almost exclusively from his work. It was as if his work had hijacked his pleasure center. At night he would lie awake fantasizing about work, not sex. And every bit of success that came his way felt more satisfying than any orgasm.

Furthermore—and this is a very important point to keep in mind when you evaluate your own sexual anhedonia—Brandon had lost joy in other closely related areas, such as spending time with his wife or children. In fact, he could not identify anything besides his work that could give him pleasure anymore.

This is the essence of sexual anhedonia. It is not just that one has no desire for sex. You might possibly have a strong sexual craving. The problem is that you can no longer enjoy it. The brain's pleasure center, which is central to sexual pleasure as well as to everything else we enjoy, has been taken over by other pleasures. By saturating this system with other, more demanding challenges, Brandon's pleasure system had become flooded and unresponsive. It is not unlike what happens in most addictions.

> This is the essence of sexual anhedonia. It is not just that one has no desire for sex . . . The problem is that you can no longer enjoy it.

I am pleased to report that through psychotherapy and Brandon's determination to overcome the problem, we were successful in helping him recover. Brandon now reports that, thankfully, his sexual pleasures are restored.

To help you determine whether you have sexual anhedonia, as well as to clarify further the nature of sexual anhedonia, I have prepared the following test:

❉

SEXUAL ANHEDONIA TEST

(Note: If you experience pain, fear, or severe anxiety over sex, this test is probably not valid for you.)

Instructions

Circle T for true or F for false for the following questions:

1. While I sometimes desire sex, it seems more like hard work than play.   T / F
2. I no longer look forward to making love and avoid the topic.   T / F
3. I used to enjoy sex, but it no longer gives me any pleasure.   T / F
4. Sex does not give me feelings of connection and sharing. T / F
5. If given the choice, I would rather read a book or watch TV than have sex.   T / F
6. I don't have to avoid thoughts about sex, because I hardly ever think about it.   T / F
7. While I used to be the one who initiates sex, I no longer take the initiative.   T / F
8. There used to be a time when I enjoyed sex more than I do now.   T / F
9. Sex has become a mechanical chore.   T / F
10. If my spouse didn't initiate sex, I probably wouldn't do so myself.   T / F
11. My work gives me more pleasure than sex.   T / F
12. I often wonder why sex was more exciting earlier in my life than now.   T / F

Scoring and Interpretation

Count the number of True responses. The maximum number is 12.

0 to 2:   You are probably free of any sexual anhedonia.

3 to 5:   Indicates some degree of sexual anhedonia.

Over 5:   Indicates a serious lack of sexual pleasure, probably due to sexual anhedonia.

DOPAMINE AND LOVE

It appears from recent research that a lack of dopamine, the brain messenger that carries signals to the brain's pleasure center, not only can cause depression (with consequent anhedonia) but also can reduce the feeling of love, which, as we all know, is a very special form of pleasure.

What has dopamine got to do with sex? We often associate love with sex or sex with love, confusing the two. So scientists recently asked the question: does a brain in love look much like a sexually stimulated brain? According to a recent CNN.com Health Report, it turns out that they are quite different though they become linked at some point through the dopamine pleasure system.[2]

People in love clearly have elevated levels of the pleasure hormone, dopamine. But there is a chicken-and-egg issue here. Which comes first: dopamine or love? Some would argue that love is a feeling, not the hormone rush of sexual arousal. No one has really figured it out yet, but I am certain that love (in the sense of a feeling) comes first, and love then pushes up the dopamine to inform the pleasure system that this is enjoyable and should be pursued. If the pleasure center gets the message, it sparks the sex hormones and lights the excitement fire.

But what happens if you have abused your pleasure system by thrilling it to death? Overdo the pursuit of pleasure, and soon your dopamine is overflooding the system, and it shuts down. There is no available dopamine for love to drive your pleasure.

It is easy to see, therefore, why high stress can make love and sex elusive. One or the other, or both, go missing in action. So it appears that we need lots of healthy dopamine not only to fall in love but also to stay in love. At the first appearance of love, dopamine increases, and then you need to maintain high dopamine to help you stay in love. So anything that interferes with dopamine, such as high stress or addictions, will also interfere with your ability to experience or, at least, to feel love.

This makes sense. The feeling of love is a form of pleasure. If you shut down the pleasure center, you also shut down your ability to feel your love. Fortunately, most of us know not to trust this lack of love feelings at times; we know we love our wives. The feeling returns again when we are over our stress. However, the idea of love needing the messenger dopamine is an intriguing one. I can imagine romance novelists having a field day with this one—if they could only understand the dopamine-love connection, it could open up a whole new genre of romance novels.

What is clear from this and other research is that people who suffer from diminished dopamine are in jeopardy of not being able to fall in love. Their feelings are blunted by the dopamine-depleted anhedonia. I am persuaded that the inability of many young men, who these days seem unable to make a long-term love attachment, may well be experiencing a stress-induced dopamine deficiency. It is certainly a topic worth researching further.

MEDICATION FOR SEXUAL ANHEDONIA

It is now becoming popular to treat several types of anhedonia with a medication that boosts the hormone dopamine—which, as we have seen, is the major neurotransmitter in the pleasure system. One such medication is an antidepressant called Wellbutrin (the generic name is bupro-prion), and you may want to consult your doctor about this. Wellbutrin is now also widely used in the treatment of a number of addiction problems, such as gambling and pornography, as a way of restoring the dopamine supply to the brain's pleasure center, especially when it has been hijacked by drugs or thrill-seeking behaviors.

> People who suffer from diminished dopamine are in jeopardy of not being able to fall in love.

Wellbutrin has also recently been shown to increase sexual desire and the intensity of sexual orgasm in women. Again, increasing dopamine, the pleasure nuerotransmitter, helps the pleasure system to work better. Not only is this good news, but it supports what I have been saying throughout this book—namely, that the high level of modern-day stress is interfering with our pleasure-giving circuits in ways that were previously unknown.

REPAIRING YOUR SEXUAL PLEASURE CENTER

While using dopamine-enhancing medications may have some reme-dial effect on sexual anhedonia, it doesn't treat the real problem—that of general overstimulation of the pleasure system. In turning to the remedial part of this chapter, I want to emphasize the importance of looking at the whole pleasure picture. This is perhaps more important in the area of sexual pleasure than in any other.

While the sexual pleasure that animals experience may come from the same basic brain mechanisms that ours do, in humans it is enriched by intimacy and love, two important higher emotional functions pro-vided by the rest of the brain. The need humans have for intimacy and love is what sets us apart from the rest of the animal kingdom. They add the delight of meaningful connections and provide a deep appreciation for having an *other* in your life. Sexual release without the other—as in masturbation—can never plumb the depths of sexual pleasure. Something is missing. Animals can neither understand nor respond to intimacy thoughts and love feelings as we can. And herein lies the secret to maximized sexual satisfaction. Even if one were to follow a life of celibacy—and many have to—the adjustments required center around finding intimacy through other relationships.

The sexual pleasure of humans stems more from higher functions of the brain than from the physiological messages carried by dopamine surges to the pleasure center. Pleasure created by a loving, sensual touch or caressing of someone you love dearly is more than just a bell ringing in the pleasure center of the brain—important as this bell is. There is much that contributes to this higher pleasure. The ingredients include knowledge about the other, physical affection and touching, craving for closeness, imagination, a total surrender of your whole person, feelings of bliss, and emotions that only the language of poets, not psychologists, can express.

> The diminutive pleasure that comes from sexual addictions and aberrations, powerful as they are in controlling behavior, falls short of genuine sexual enchantment.

This is where the diminutive pleasure that comes from sexual addictions and aberrations, powerful as they are in controlling behavior, falls short of genuine sexual enchantment. Predatory sexual pleasure, including one-night stands or loveless, random sex, is hollow and unfulfilling. There can never be a feeling of deep satisfaction and contentment, let alone happiness, when one uses another for physical sexual gratification.

Why does physical sex fall so short of real, deeply satisfying pleasure? Because it is derived only from the skeleton of the brain's pleasure system, not from its total body. Physical sexual pleasure lacks intensity and deep satisfaction because it is nothing more than animal pleasure. You might as well be a dog. Now don't misunderstand me. I love my dog. As I mentioned earlier, he is the source of much joy to me. But he knows nothing of the deeper life and glorious affection I have for my wife and the profound pleasure she provides because of this.

> To be restricted to the physical realm of pleasure is to restrict your pleasure.

To be restricted to the physical realm of pleasure is to restrict your pleasure. To be fully human, you have to embrace with depth of feeling and love all that your whole mind can offer. This is what provides seventh-heaven pleasure, rich and deeply satisfying.

BUILDING HEALTHIER SEXUAL PLEASURES

Restoring your lost intimacy and rekindling your desire and enjoyment of sex may require the help of a psychologist or family therapist who specializes in sex therapy. It would be misleading for me to suggest that this is a problem that can easily be fixed by a self-help approach. The problem of low sexual desire, especially if you have been experiencing it for a while, can have serious consequences for marriage.

So while I cannot offer a quick self-help fix, there are two areas I can help you with here. First, many sexual distortions originate in the long waiting years between the onset of puberty and the time when one is married and ready to raise a family. The distortions arise because, unwittingly, we learn to connect our adrenaline arousal system (which is an *emergency* system) with our normal sexual hormone arousal. In other words, we come to look for exciting extras for sexual stimulation. When, for example, you engage in risky or out of the ordinary sexual behavior, the release of adrenaline adds excitement.[3]

For instance, the early sexual experiences of most men occur when they masturbate while looking at a porn magazine. Many men report that they inadvertently found the magazine in their father's drawer or desk. Since there is an element of fear attached at being found out or doing something naughty, a massive surge of adrenaline floods the body, adding excitement to sexual feelings. The problem is that it gives your sexual feelings a tremendous lift. Adrenaline adds an element of excitement that is not normally present in sexual arousal—or at least it shouldn't be. After a while, men get used to this *extra* sexual excitement coming from doing something sexual that is risky, and soon it becomes a habit, even an addiction.

> You need to learn that healthy sexual arousal doesn't need any extra excitement to be enjoyable.

It is this pairing of adrenaline with sexual arousal that is the major cause of sexual distortion in our day. The sexual-adrenaline connection also leads to sexual perversions such as adding pain to sex (sexual sadism and masochism) and, most seriously, rape (a crime that produces high-octane adrenaline).

I regret to say that little attention has been given to how male sexuality has been grossly distorted by this pairing of sex to adrenaline. Aside from addressing it in my own writings, I am not aware of any formal research into the phenomenon. It's almost as if our culture has come to the place where it legitimizes the use of as much adrenaline excitement as one can get out of sex. Unfortunately, women pay the price for this distortion.

To heal your sexual distortions (and this is more a male problem than a female one), this pairing of adrenaline with sexual arousal has to be broken. You need to learn that healthy sexual arousal doesn't need any extra excitement to be enjoyable. In fact, over the long haul, it actually reduces your pleasure.

I don't mean to imply that sexuality should never get any help from other factors. Obviously, there are healthy ways to bring out your sexual pleasure and make it more meaningful. Husbands, try being a bit more romantic around the house (after all, sex starts in the kitchen). Take home flowers occasionally. Or help put the kids to bed. For both partners, build a stronger emotional connection. Have regular date nights when candles and a special dinner are the spices that enhance the flavor of your sexual relationship.

You also need to remove some of the powerful adrenaline spices you have become accustomed to adding to your sexual experience. How can you do this? Here are a few suggestions:

* Try to focus more on your relationship with your partner, not the sex itself. Intimacy with your spouse is what really brings out superb pleasure.

* Avoid using external sources of stimulation, such as pornography or fantasies about someone else. The more you rely on these external mechanisms of arousal, the more you become dependent on them—and the further you move from the intimacy of your loved one.

* Do not push your partner into unusual practices just to fuel your need for adrenaline excitement. Of course, some experimentation is part of learning the techniques of intercourse. But distorted

sexuality often wants to explore the bizarre and unnatural. If your partner feels uncomfortable, you will rob pleasure for both of you.

* If you depend on adrenal arousal for sex, you may also depend on adrenaline for a lot of other things as well and could possibly be addicted to it—so break your broad addiction to adrenaline as well by reducing risk taking or seeking stimulation through adrenaline activity.

Second, your sexual pleasure system can easily be hijacked by over-stimulated conditioning to unreal sexual stimuli. This is the problem with explicit external sexual stimuli, such as pornography or romantic novels. These present a distorted perspective of romance and sexuality that is pure fiction, designed to entertain, and has nothing to do with real life. They also present unrealistic images of both men and women, and no partner can ever expect to live up to fictitious characters.

> Sexual pleasure is ultimately all about the quality of your relationship with your partner.

The solution to breaking these habits lies in not feeding your sexual appetite with them. By minimizing the use of artificial sexual stimulants, you may at first feel that you have thrown the baby out with the bathwater and done away with all sexual pleasure. But trust me here. Resting your sexual taste buds for a while will restore your sexual pleasure to its full grandeur again.

I can also tell you this: sexual pleasure does not come from your gonads; it comes from your whole being. The pot of gold is found at the end of the relationship rainbow—nowhere else. Sexual pleasure is ultimately all about the quality of your relationship with your partner.

SEVEN STEPS *to* RECOVERING YOUR PLEASURE

STEP 1—SEEK THE RIGHT FORM OF PLEASURE

One can get just as much exultation in losing oneself
in a little thing as in a big thing. It is nice to think
how one can be recklessly lost in a daisy.
—ANNE MORROW LINDBERGH

Maintaining a healthy and robust pleasure system begins with evaluating and changing your basic lifestyle habits. Most importantly, you have to redirect your life and pursue the right forms of pleasure. All demolishers of pleasure come from activities that flood the dopamine neurotransmitter that tells the brain what should and shouldn't give pleasure.

But it is not only big pleasures that can rob us of joy. You can just as easily misuse some of the basic innate pleasures of your body and mind, as well as your relationships. The key to maintaining a healthy pleasure system is to make sure you seek the right sort of pleasure.

As I have indicated, there are many types of pleasure. Some are conducive to mental, physical, and spiritual health; others are not. Some actually help to boost your experience of pleasure by enhancing your underlying happiness and contentment, while others create longings and addictions that hijack the pleasure system. In this chapter, I will present several exercises designed to boost the right sort of pleasure.

TYPES OF PLEASURE

It is quite evident from my observations that there are several types of pleasure. For the sake of simplicity, I have reduced them to two basic types: type A pleasure and type B pleasure. These go in line with the well-known type A and type B personality types. However, while there may be a link between type A pleasure and the characteristics of the type A personality, don't view them as the same thing. Type B personalities can easily get caught up in type A pleasure pursuits and vice versa.

> The key to maintaining a healthy pleasure system is to make sure you seek the right sort of pleasure.

Type A Pleasure Seekers

Originally, the type A personality was linked with early heart disease. Its full name is the *Type A Coronary Prone Personality*. The characteristics of the type A personality revolve around haste and anger. These personality types are often described as *time-urgent* or *time-impatient* people.

I am a classic type A personality. People like me are always in a hurry—we eat fast, talk fast, and work fast. As a result, we are also impatient with delays. We tend toward a free-floating hostility—in other words, we quickly get angry. And it is these characteristics that put us at risk for early heart disease and heart attacks.

Type A personalities love type A pleasures and derive an enormous thrill from adrenaline-driven activities. So they seek out exciting behaviors in order to maintain a pleasurable state of arousal. In every respect, type A personalities are adrenaline junkies, and this high level of stimulation inevitably shuts down easy access to the pleasure center.

What are the consequences of pursuing type A pleasures?

* Maxes out pathways leading to pleasure center.
* Leads to addictive behaviors by overstimulating the pleasure system.
* Creates an addictive process that needs ever-increasing levels of pleasure.
* Undermines the ability to be enduringly happy.
* Depletes natural brain tranquilizers (increases anxiety).
* Depletes the immune system (deteriorates health).
* Depletes natural endorphins (lowers tolerance for pain).
* Creates a state of anhedonia (self-defeating pleasure system).

Clearly, there is a price to be paid for being a type A pleasure addict.

Type B Pleasure Seekers

Type B personalities are in all respects the opposite. They are slow to get angry, easygoing in general, and not as time conscious. They prefer type B pleasures and derive joy from being low-keyed, not adrenaline-driven. In fact, they do not enjoy being high on adrenaline at all because it gives them

TYPE A PLEASURES

- Crave over-the-top experiences
- Require urgent and heightened arousal
- Feed the adrenaline-hungry person
- Rely on high excitement and thrilling adventure
- Want more action, louder music, extreme thrilling sports

the jitters and makes them edgy. At times when I am low-keyed, I feel this way as well—but it is rare.

So what do the two pleasure types look like, and how can this information point us toward building a healthier pleasure system?

PURSUING HEALTHIER PLEASURES

One way to amend your pleasure system is to focus on pursuing more type B pleasures—especially if you are a dyed-in-the-wool type A personality. Type B pleasures can provide many benefits, no matter what your personality style. Here are just a few:

* Enhance your feelings of well-being

* Lower your stress level

* Enable biological flexibility—greater overall physical and mental health

* Enable you to achieve a higher level of enduring happiness

* Help to heal traumatic or psychological pain (is a great comforter)

* Increase your *hedonic tone* (improve your pleasure response by *toning up* the pleasure system)

* Reverse any anhedonia that may have developed

It stands to reason, therefore, that pursuing type B pleasures can help to prevent anhedonia. I have seen many depressed clients who have been able to keep their emotional numbness to a minimum simply because they had developed an appreciation for the joyfulness that type B pleasures could provide before they became depressed.

The pursuit of healthy passions gives us meaning and purpose in life because they naturally hit the spot in our pleasure system. These pursuits express our natural talents. You can't live a full life without them.

In the movie *Chariots of Fire*, the Olympic runner Eric Little expressed this concept beautifully when he said, "When I run, I feel God's pleasure." And this is true. We feel the deepest of pleasures when we are fully engaged in our innate, authentic uniqueness—our passions and purpose. Find your own; don't borrow from others. Make it a priority to find and grow your own healthy passions.

❋

TYPE B PLEASURES

- Derive mainly from natural experiences that help to lower our stress hormones
- Provide deeply satisfying enjoyment and happiness
- Play the pleasure game according to nature's rules by staying within the boundaries of healthy pleasure
- Tolerate short excursions into high levels of stimulating pleasure because the system remains healthy and recovers quickly
- Provide short bursts of high-adrenaline excitement that can be therapeutic
- Come more from natural activities (such as eating healthy food, exercising, enjoying the little things of life) than from artificially created excitement

THE DANGER OF MISGUIDED PLEASURES

Sex can be fun, chocolate tastes good, and shopping can be exciting. The adrenaline rush from extreme sports, the thrill of cheering on spectator sports, and similar pleasure pursuits are not necessarily bad for us. But they can be misused, bringing only temporary bursts of gratification and often lasting negative results. Even the smartest, most God-fearing people in the Bible, like King David and Samson, were vulnerable to the temptation of misdirected pleasure, making them do unwise things. When we are vulnerable and give in to unauthentic pleasure, we pursue it irrationally, justifying the behavior. "I want what I want, and I want it now, my way." This is part of the human dilemma.

> We feel the deepest of pleasures when we are fully engaged in our innate, authentic uniqueness—our passions and purpose.

Giving in to small, misguided pleasures can lead to even worse consequences like drug addiction, loveless marriage, and gluttony. These are indisputably destructive to our lives, our pleasure center, and to those around us.

LOOKING FOR PLEASURE IN
ALL THE WRONG PLACES

We all need to know where we are vulnerable to unhealthy pleasure—where our pleasure centers can easily be hijacked. Knowing where the dangers lie in the pleasure minefield can help us to focus on the right sources of pleasure.

While some of these mines are specific to each of us (one danger for you may not be a danger for me), there are some unhealthy behaviors or relationships that are guaranteed to be pleasure busters in your life. Pleasure busters can overpower healthy sources of happiness. They can be behaviors or habits that are guaranteed to derail and tear down your pleasure center. They may seem somewhat harmless on the surface, but they will definitely prevent your brain from receiving healthy, authentic pleasure and reward fulfillment.

One common pleasure buster is the idea that you should *go fast and hard*. By upping the pace and intensity of activities in your life, you try to get more pleasure out of them. It is a sad fact that modern, success-driven life disparages calmness and contentment—the simple pleasures of life. Taking life too casually is often viewed as complacency or even downright laziness. "Content-ment encourages slothfulness and doesn't achieve something great," a client once stated. "You've got to be pushing yourself to the edge, controlling every moment of every day, filling every opportunity with motivational impetus, else your life will be unhappy, and you'll end up a nobody." Yes, this man was a type A adrenaline junkie. And his drivenness became his Achilles' heel. He became a deeply depressed, unhappy person. Nothing seemed to help him.

> Knowing where the dangers lie in the pleasure minefield can help us to focus on the right sources of pleasure.

So besides being aware of shortcuts and fast-track misguided path-ways to pleasure, also beware of the pleasure busters in your life. Some of the common pleasure busters for all of us include:

* Being around negative friends or family members
* Working in a job that is unsatisfying

* Making poor choices for your life

* Neglecting your self-care

* Eating unhealthy food

* Not exercising enough for your age and health

* Allowing too much stress in your life

* Practicing unhealthy sleep habits

* Neglecting your self-care

* Living in the fast lane

No doubt you can add many, many more pleasure busters to this list.

PLEASURE BOOSTERS

As opposed to having pleasure busters in your life, you can also develop pleasure boosters—behaviors or habits that can effectively boost your experience of healthy pleasures. The following are some breakthrough strategies that can help you develop some of the more important pleasure boosters.

Pleasure Booster #1—Getting Enough Sleep

Believe it or not, if you are not getting enough sleep, you'll definitely be looking for pleasure in all the wrong places.

There is much confusion about sleep today. It is a topic that always generates a lot of discussion at any seminar I teach. Do we sleep too much? Do we sleep too little? Let me summarize for you some basic information from a recent series of articles published by the American Psychological Association.

* Why do we sleep? Because the brain, like the rest of the body, needs rest.

* When we don't get enough sleep, our body will force us to make up for it.

* Sleep helps the brain to fix new memories and replenish energy.

* Sleep helps to consolidate new memories.

* The more sleep we get, the faster we can perform many mental tasks.

* Sleep helps us retain new memories (learn new things).

* Sleep helps the brain make new connections.

* Dream sleep is the *defragmentation* program of the brain.

* Sleep helps the growth of new brain cells.

* Good sleep helps to undo the effects of stress.[1]

If sleep does all this for us, why do we fight it? Why would we not want to sleep more? And this brings me to the all-important question: how much sleep do we really need?

Let me warn you not to pay too much attention to some newspaper reports about too much sleep reducing longevity. According to the report of the President's Commission on Sleep, the minimum sleep needed for a healthy adult is about eight and a half hours a night.[2] I claim it has to be nine hours because we really sleep in cycles of ninety minutes, and this multiplies to nine hours. Twenty-five years ago, I

> Getting adequate sleep on a regular basis will help enormously to build a healthy pleasure-boosting system.

changed my sleep habits from five hours a night to nine hours—and the difference it made to my life was tremendous. My blood pressure dropped, I felt happier, and my energy level jumped up. Try sleeping longer, and I guarantee you will feel better, and your brain, including your pleasure center, will work better too.

Here are some essential rules for good sleeping:

1. Always go to bed and wake up at the same time every day. Your brain uses an internal clock that needs to be reset daily.

2. Darken your environment at least an hour before you go to bed, like using low-level lighting. It helps release melatonin that puts you to sleep.

3. Avoid all stimulants such as caffeine after 3:00 p.m. Caffeine interferes with your sleep architecture.

4. Avoid using alcohol to put you to sleep. The effect wears off quickly, and you get rebound wakefulness.

5. If you live in a noisy environment, use earplugs to dampen the sound.

6. Make sure you get a good physical workout every day. Physical fatigue helps your body to sleep better.

7. When you go to bed, use a notebook to write down any unfinished tasks or unresolved conflicts bothering you. Putting it down on paper helps your brain to let it go.

8. Try not to use an alarm to wake you. By all means, set an alarm as backup, but try to get to bed early enough so that you wake up naturally. This way you know you're getting enough sleep. Being awakened during the last dream of

the night is like turning off your computer in the middle of its defragmentation—you create chaos.

Getting adequate sleep on a regular basis will help enormously to build a healthy pleasure-boosting system. Pleasant dreams!

Pleasure Booster #2—Practicing Self-Care

Doesn't it seem like life is getting faster and faster? It's becoming more and more difficult to find time just to *be*. Our hurriedness robs us of the opportunity to relax, rejuvenate, and enjoy the simple pleasures in life. There is little time for self-nurturing. Unless you are intentional and make a determined effort, you are not going to be self-caring. This could lose you the game of life.

Recent media surveys reveal that we are paying the price for this lack of self-care.[3] Many today lament not being able to make time for self-care, even if they see it as a priority. Women, especially, long for deeper meaning in their lives—they would welcome the blessing of a little joy, a modest peace of mind, and a sense of purpose that goes beyond meeting family obligations, running errands, caregiving, and getting through half the chores on the checklist. Many women feel like they are forever fulfilling everyone else's expectations and few of their own. In the process, they clog the natural pathways to their pleasure centers.

> Unless you are intentional and make a determined effort, you are not going to be self-caring.

Why do women, in particular, neglect their own self-care so readily? The primary culprit is their natural nurturing tendencies. Many women pour themselves into nurturing others, neglecting care of themselves. Women often overfunction by doing too much. They do not set good boundaries because they feel guilty when saying no. Then there is also the fear of competition and failure. Unresolved emotions like anger also cause many women to give up on themselves. When women are fearful, conflicted, angry, resentful, and despairing, they easily block out their pleasure center, robbing themselves of even the simplest delights that life has to offer. Men usually don't seem to have such problems.

Is there a solution to the challenge of finding time for self-care? I believe there is. It's finding "me" time. And it is as important for men as it is for women—so men, don't jump to the next section.

"For your mental, physical, and psychological well-being, you sometimes just need to stop," states a recent CNN Health report. "Then you need to do something you want to do. You need to take some Me Time."[4] What wise counsel.

In the study reported in this article, people were asked what they wanted more of in their lives; the two most common responses were *peace* and *time*. No surprises here. We all long for serenity and balance—and more time to do what we want to do.

How can you claim more "me" time? Here are some helpful strategies.

1. Make it a priority to find time. Finding time for yourself has to be intentional—you have to make it a priority equal to, if not higher than, everything else in your life. If you struggle to give yourself permission to take time out for yourself, you may want to read up on the topic to understand its value to your mind and health, and to your ability to care for others. Remember the advice flight attendants give to passengers before takeoff: "In the event of losing cabin pressure, first put the oxygen mask on yourself—then help others."

    Mark your "me" time on your calendar with ink, so it cannot

be erased. No going back! Keep your promises to yourself just as you keep them to others, and treat your "me" time like any other important priority.

2. Get some peace and quiet. Unfortunately, I have many clients who have followed through and claimed "me" time—only to then use the time to complete some project or run errands. "Me" time is for peace and quiet. So every so often, unplug your phone or switch off the cell and take some time out for solitude, reflection, and renewal.

3. Do something you like to do—not what you have to do— every day. Explore what you are passionate about—what brings you alive—and clear a healthy pathway to your pleasure center.

4. Find an activity that serves as an escape valve to let off steam. Explore what kinds of activities give you a sense of release and rejuvenation. If a book group doesn't appeal to you, maybe an art class will. Some find that volunteer work provides a soul-enriching sense of accomplishment; for others, it is too draining. A lot depends on the stage of life you are in. A young mother may need to get away from children during her "me" time while an empty-nest mother may enjoy volunteering at a school to be around children.

Pleasure Booster #3—Eating for the Right Reasons

What does eating have to do with anhedonia? Many misguided pleasures come from our natural desires—powerful drives that can be misused or become substitutes for other human needs. Overindulging ourselves in what seems pleasurable can bring unhappiness. The most basic of human pleasures, such as food, love, and sex, can become misguided pleasures. I've addressed love and sex elsewhere, so let's look here at how food becomes a misguided pleasure.

Tasting, eating, and drinking are among the most powerful rewards our pleasure center is programmed to receive. This is true for both animals and humans, which explains a lot about my puppy's obsession with food. The right tidbits can send him into puppy seventh heaven. Any sort of fish—fresh or canned—drives him crazy with delight. He jumps all over you, and if he were not such a small dog, he could easily overcome you just to get at that piece of fish you are holding.

> Overindulging ourselves in what seems pleasurable can bring unhappiness.

Why does food have such strong power over us? The simple answer is that our survival depends on it, so the body gives it a high priority. We need food to provide the fuel and energy needed for survival. Amazingly, our taste and smell sensors have direct access to our pleasure center, opening wide the gates to ecstasy.

MOUTH EATING VERSUS EMOTIONAL EATING

Emotional eating, as opposed to mouth eating, is a form of abuse to the brain's pleasure system. It's not effective therapy, not healthy for you, and can lead to obesity, food addictions, and cravings, if you overdo it. If emotional eating seems to be a problem area for you, I advise you to get professional help with a counselor or program that deals with emotions and food disorders.

The following test will help you discover whether emotional eating is interfering with your life and health:

EMOTIONAL EATING INVENTORY

Instructions

Use the following scale to score your answer to each question:

0 = Never or rarely

1 = Occasionally (several times a month)

2 = Often (several times a week)

3 = Always

Score

1. I feel that my eating is out of control. _____

2. There are times when I crave certain foods that I know are not good for me. _____

3. I want to eat even when I am not physically hungry. _____

4. When I am feeling really low, I find that good food will lift my spirit. _____

5. Food is on my mind a lot, and I even dream about it. _____

6. I tend to eat more food when I am under a lot of stress. _____

7. I tend to eat fast, so I cannot really savor the taste. _____

8. I struggle with my weight and have difficulty keeping it in a healthy range. _____

9. When I get hungry, my body goes crazy and I become very irritable. _____

10. I am not proud of the way food dominates my life. _____

Total _____

Scoring and Interpretation

Total the score given to each question. The highest possible score is 30.

0 to 5: Indicates little or no emotional eating.

6 to 10: You probably have some emotional eating.

11 to 20: Indicates clear emotional eating tendencies.

Over 20: Your emotional eating is a severe problem, and you may need professional help.

The pleasure of eating is often misused to pacify our mood or to fill what feels like an empty void. Sometimes emotional eating is used to calm our nerves, satisfy a deep longing for something missing in our lives, or just for the sheer pleasure of overindulging.

The solution lies in eating for the right reasons and then developing healthier eating habits. Since painful moods are powerful in their ability to misdirect your eating, you need to first address any emotional disorder in your life. Seek a psychologist or psychotherapist and deal with the underlying cause. And then train yourself in eating foods that are nutritious, healthy, and tasteful. There is an enormous amount of help available on the Internet, so there is little point in my repeating it here. Start by looking at the Internet resources provided in appendix B. They will provide links to many other resources as well.

STEP 2—RECAPTURE THE JOY OF LITTLE THINGS

Pleasures lie thickest where no pleasures seem;
There's not a leaf that falls upon the ground
But holds some joy of silence or of sound,
Some sprite begotten of a summer dream.
—Laman Blanchard, Sonnet VII, "Hidden Joys"

D o you remember how much pleasure simple things gave you as a child? The Christmas gift you really wanted. A trip to the zoo or a park. The joy of seeing the ocean for the first time (I grew up 400 miles inland from the ocean).

I can remember with great delight many of the fragrances from my childhood—orange blossoms in the springtime, my grandmother's homemade dried fruit, and the smell of a neighbor's honeysuckle bush. I can also remember the muddy smell of the river that I spent much of my childhood swimming in. Then there was the whiff of dried cow manure that my grandfather would collect from the open veld to grow his tomatoes. And I can't forget the medicinal aroma of eucalyptus trees that made up the large plantations, grown by the gold mining companies for underground tunnel support.

I can also remember the tender touch of my wife's fingers the first time we held hands. Of course, those were the days when holding hands was the first step in the dating process. If a girl held your hand, you knew you had made a catch. I was too shy to initiate that touch, but the young lady who was to become my wife took care of that.

> Overwhelmingly, people report their most enduring and meaningful pleasures come from relatively minor, ordinary things in their lives.

What is somewhat alarming is that these little things from my early life were able to deliver more pleasure than most things in my life today. Yes, anhedonia has taken its toll in my life also.

THE BEST PLEASURES OF ALL

Because I have always been captive to the notion that the best pleasures come from the simple things of life, I thought I'd do a little Internet research to see what other people find to be pleasure giving. I was amazed how easy the exercise was—and how much information I found. In fact, this might be a great exercise for you to do yourself. Go to an Internet search engine (if you're not sure how, ask any person under the age of thirty) and type in "What things really give you pleasure." Then take a moment to read the responses. One Web site listed more than sixteen pages of simple things people find pleasurable.

Here are a few examples of things people listed as their simple pleasures:

* Walking through the park in the early evening
* Sitting on the porch with friends
* Burning a candle with a favorite scent
* Sleeping on a cool pillow on a hot night
* Going barefoot after a rain and having mud squish between my toes
* The smell of baking bread
* When my wife snorts with laughter
* Petting my cat

If you make a list of the things that give you the most pleasure, you will likely find that your list has much in common with these kinds of responses. Notice that they all emphasize that the best pleasures of all come from the little things in your life. In fact, scores of the respondents said things like:

* The little things are what make life bearable.
* My little things are always better than my big things.
* Without little pleasures, my life wouldn't be worth living.

Overwhelmingly, people report their most enduring and meaningful pleasures come from relatively minor, ordinary things in their lives. So why is it then that we make more effort and spend more money looking for happiness in the *big* things of life?

❖ BEING THANKFUL FOR LITTLE BLESSINGS

Besides trying to find pleasure in most everything you do, the little pleasures in your life should never be ignored. In fact, you should be more intentional about appreciating these happy places in your life—they help to distract and restore hope and faith. Here are a few simple pleasures others have found to be truly satisfying and pleasurable:

- Reading a good book
- Arranging a beautiful bouquet
- Getting a relaxation massage
- Talking and sharing with a friend
- Having a good laugh
- Eating fresh baked bread
- Getting a good parking spot
- Golfing on a freshly mowed lawn

THE EIFFEL TOWER OR A BABY HORSE?

One illustration that makes my point here comes from a family incident. About twelve yeas ago, my middle daughter, the mother of two of my grandsons, was widowed when her husband was killed in an automobile accident. It was a devastating experience for the whole family and, as you can imagine, deeply impacted my two grandsons. So several summers later, I decided to take my daughter and grandsons to Europe to lift their spirits. I had traveled there extensively and wanted them to catch the travel bug as well. Traveling light with just backpacks, we set off from London with train passes and no fixed agenda. We would visit whatever struck our fancy.

It was a fantastically healing experience for all of us. We visited all the popular attractions—the Eiffel Tower in Paris, the Coliseum in Rome, fantastic castles on the Rhine, Alpine villages in Switzerland.

About halfway through our hectic trip, we took a break and stopped over for a couple of days in a four-hundred-year-old guesthouse on a hillside above Lake Thun in Switzerland. It was in the middle of nowhere, far from the tourist crush and surrounded by cows. I had visited this place several times and had fallen in love with it, yet I feared that it was not likely to excite my teenage grandsons. But we needed a day and night of good rest before charging off to the next European attraction, and this place was as good as any.

We arrived at the guesthouse late in the afternoon. It was overcast and a bit chilly. The boys were restless, so my daughter and I decided to take them for a little walk into the Swiss countryside. Everywhere we looked, we could see Swiss cows and farmers puttering around.

As we turned a corner, we came across an open field. A horse and a relatively newborn foal were grazing together behind a single electrified wire. Since the grass inside the fence area had been well grazed,

- Doing an intentional act of kindness
- Taking a trip to a new place
- Rejoicing when your team wins
- Christmas decorations and music
- Looking at the stars at night
- Watching the sunset
- Finding the perfect gift
- Preparing a tasty meal
- Watching Monday night football
- Working hard for a good cause
- Seeing an answer to prayer
- Finding low-calorie chocolate
- Being absorbed and fulfilled
- Meeting someone new
- Getting a good seat on the plane
- Looking through old photos
- Learning to do something new
- Riding with the windows down

the foal was struggling to reach fresh grass on the other side of the fence. My grandsons ran up to the fence, grabbed handfuls of the long grass on their side, and gingerly offered the grass to the foal—avoiding the potential shock from the fence themselves. Immediately, the foal bonded with them. For the next half an hour, the boys had fun feeding the foal until it was time for us to return to the guesthouse for dinner.

Early the next morning, we were on the train to the next busy tourist location. Not knowing what sort of sites would excite my grandsons, I had planned our trip so that we would have a few days of unscheduled time on our way back to London. So as we came to the last few days, I gave the boys the opportunity to choose their most favorite place so we could go back to it as we traveled back to London for our flight back to the US.

> By discovering and reexperiencing past pleasures, you can open up an enormous source of healing for a damaged pleasure system.

What would be their choice? I wondered. The Eiffel Tower? The Eiger or Jungfrau? The Coliseum? Or perhaps Buckingham Palace? They were free to choose whatever they wanted to see again before we ended the trip. Without even blinking an eye, both boys asked if we could go back and feed the foal in the little village of Einegan. I was flummoxed. Then I remembered that even with teenagers who usually demand intense excitement, it is the simple things that provide the purest of pleasures.

So we set aside palaces, towers, and ancient ruins to spend our last days feeding a foal we had fallen in love with on a Swiss hillside far away from the tourist track. What a lesson for all of us. The little things of life offer more pleasure than the big.

DISCOVERING YOUR PLEASURABLE PAST

By discovering and reexperiencing past pleasures, you can open up an enormous source of healing for a damaged pleasure system. A bit of regression to an earlier time in your life can be very therapeutic. The process of recovering some of these memories can build your pleasure by stirring up pleasure connections you made a long, long time ago.

A good place to start is by opening up earlier happy memories. Take a moment to do an inventory of some of the early joys in your life. Try to recall what stage in your life was the happiest for you. Was it at school, high school, and college or beyond? Can you recall what specific activities created the happiness? Sports? Hobbies? Friends? Extracurricular activities?

Recall some of these happy events and journal them. Journaling is a great way to leave a history of your life for your kids. My wife and I have even started to tape-record some of these events to pass on to our children as we build a record of our family history.

After you have jotted down some joyful events, then reflect on the following questions: When did this all change? Did you get too busy? Did you lose some of your joy when you got married and had to raise kids? Did your joy fade as you spent more time building a career or meeting financial needs?

There are some memories from your childhood that should never be dumped. Cling to them with all the tenacity you can muster. They are the bits and pieces that can contribute to building true happiness for you, even when it seems you have lost all ability to be happy.

> Even though you may be anhedonic now, you can still recapture a lot of your childlike joy by revisiting your childhood happiness memories.

Well, what am I leading up to here? Simply this: even though you may be anhedonic now, you can still recapture a lot of your childlike joy by revisiting your childhood happiness memories. I've done this all my adult life and found that in times when I am really down in the dumps, it helps to put my unhappiness into a larger perspective. *Yes*, I will say to myself, *right now I am feeling unhappy, even miserable. But I remember when* . . . Looking back at happy times in my life, including in my earliest childhood, lifts my spirit. Recapturing childhood joy actually helps to restore missing adult pleasure.

HOW DOES EXPLORING PAST PLEASURES WORK?

How does this process of exploring past pleasures work? Recalling childhood pleasure revitalizes dormant memories, and by recirculating them through the memory system of your brain, you help to reset the brain's pleasure registry. This can offset unhappy or anhedonic states that are robbing you of pleasure now. It's not unlike what you do when your computer's memory has become contaminated and you select *system restore*. The computer resets itself to what it was at a previous date when its memory was uncontaminated. Relive happy childhood events, and you can do the same for your brain.

Allow me to illustrate this process with a personal example, and then I will give you a series of simple exercises that can help you to do the same.

This story concerns my grandfather, whose name I bear and whom I loved dearly. My grandparents lived in a small country village on the Vaal River in South Africa. On hot summer evenings, we would sit on the front veranda of their home—Grandma would be crocheting, an elderly aunt who took care of them would knit, and my younger brother and I would sit on the wall of the *stoep* (which means *porch*) while my grandfather would enthrall us with stories of his escapades as a young soldier at the end of the 1800s, before he married my grandmother.

The only entertainment we had in those days came from a short-wave radio. If you fiddled with its knobs long enough, you could hear a distant radio station from Mozambique a thousand miles away. So there was really nothing else to do on hot, summer evenings but sit on the front stoop and enjoy my grandfather's stories. And what a wonderfully happy time it was. All day I would anticipate the evening when, after

> Using your memory of past pleasures provides emotional healing like nothing else for the present.

dinner, we would take our places on the front porch, turn out the lights to chase away the mosquitoes, and wait for my grandfather to light his pipe and start his stories.

As a soldier in 1899, my grandfather traveled the length and breadth of southern Africa on horseback, camping in the middle of what was then wild country. He had shot several lions and other wild animals (for his own protection, he assured me), and their skins served as rugs that adorned his house and proof that he was not fabricating the stories. Each evening he would tell a different story, and most of them I can remember to this day.

Many of my grandfather's stories were about South African history, a history he helped to shape. How he went on a two-thousand-mile expedition to what became known as *Rhodesia* (named after Cecil Rhodes, the governor of the Cape in the late 1890s). How, during the Boer War, he helped relieve the siege of Mafeking and then the siege of Kimberly, where his young wife and my father, still just a baby, were hiding deep within the hole of the Kimberly diamond mine.

I can't vouch for the veracity of every story he told although I couldn't imagine why he would tell me fibs with my grandmother sitting right there and adding missing details. But the joy I experience as an adult in revisiting those stories is indescribable. And I was also awed by my grandfather's medals—one for every one of the campaigns he described and inscribed with his name. A real, live history book displayed before my eyes. Later in school, when the history lesson covered events that my grandfather was a part of, I could elaborate for the class and add some of the details I had received firsthand from my grandfather. What joy!

Here again, even as I retell this story for you, I experience the same joyful pleasure as I did all those years ago. By recapturing past pleasures, you help to revitalize dormant memories. By recirculating them through the memory system of your brain, they open up new joys. There is a powerful and persistent connection between your pleasure center and your memory. Using your memory of past pleasures provides emotional healing like nothing else for the present.

EXERCISES IN RELIVING PLEASURABLE MEMORIES

The following series of exercises can help you recover the joy of the simple things in your life by recovering happy childhood memories. These exercises can be very helpful in restoring your pleasure system.

Exercise 1: Set Aside Your Unhappy Memories

Before you attempt to recover happy childhood memories, you need to acknowledge that not all childhood memories are happy and intentionally set aside the negative ones, else they will intrude and undermine the happy ones. Some of my readers may, in fact, have been severely traumatized as children. And this doesn't end with childhood. Many horrible things can happen to ordinary people every day.

So it is important for this exercise that you try to set aside any unhappy memories that arise while exploring your childhood. This exercise is not about reliving bad times in order to eradicate them from your memory. In fact, psychologists no longer believe that reliving trauma has any benefit at all. All it does is rehearse the trauma and entrench it further in the part of the brain called the amygdala, which is responsible for remembering bad things so as to help us avoid them in the future. No, while the objective facts about bad events need to be remembered, reexperiencing pain doesn't help.

So for starters, get a notebook and create a list of all the negative experiences of your childhood. It can be a very brief summary—such as "my parents' divorce" or "the day Billy died." Writing down these bad memories externalizes them and helps you set them aside—that is, get them out of your head and into a permanent form of memory (i.e., your notebook). In a sense, recording these experiences removes the nagging tendency of your brain to remind you of the bad things so as to prevent them from occurring again. Then just set this list aside. We have more important memories to focus on.

Exercise 2: Recall Happy Memories

Now that you have identified your past negative memories, make a list of positive memories of happy events from your past. You will use this list to prompt you with happy memories as you proceed with the exercise. So try to recall, in general terms, happy events from earlier in your life. You need not focus on the details as you will try to discover them later. Just list potential memories worthy of exploration.

For instance, when I did this exercise, my list included the following: "Going fishing with Granddad; helping Dad build a wood lathe; climbing large oak trees down the street; the first taste of homemade ice cream; the smell of the earth after an African thunderstorm." As you start this process, additional memories will come to mind—so write them down. This list will be the agenda for the rest of the exercise.

Exercise 3: Recreate and Reexperience Previous Happy Times

Now with this list in mind, whenever you have some time to yourself, such as when waiting to fall asleep, riding the bus to school or work, or when the rest of the family is watching TV, choose one of these happy events and try to recreate as many details as you can.

At first, you may not be able to recall very much. Memories have to be teased out of your brain. One leads to another as your memory opens up through associations. And even when you are not actually thinking about your childhood memories, they will spring to mind. After a while, you will be quite surprised just how much you are able to recall from happy events in your early childhood when you focus on them.

Exercise 4: Add Memory Feelings

You not only can recreate the memories of happier times but you can also recover the feelings associated with the events. This is important. Don't just try to recall the facts of these events. This can be a starting point, but try to recall the feelings you experienced at the time. You might also be able to remember certain smells or even tastes associated with these memories. I can recall the first taste of a neighbor's homemade ice cream. How I wish I could recreate that taste in my ice cream maker today.

Hang on to these feelings, smells, and tastes as long as you can—savoring and enjoying them. Then, at a later time, try remembering them again. Once you have them well ensconced in your current memory, they will be a source of happiness that is able to rejuvenate your pleasure center.

It may take a while to recapture joyful events from earlier in your life, but in the course of time it will get easier. And your capacity for enjoying the simple things in your life—not just from the past, but in the present as well—will grow. And don't forget that journaling these memories can help to entrench them even further.

CAPTURING THE SIMPLE JOY OF THE PRESENT

While recycling the memories of past positive events can bring a measure of healing to your anhedonia, you need also to work on capturing the simple joys of the here-and-now. Being able to savor the joy of the present moment is as important as being able to recapture joy from your past. In fact, it is more important. We let an awful lot of *now joy* pass us by. We are often too busy to notice the joy of this moment.

My wife and I know two wonderful songwriters whose words and music have been a joy to us for many years. One of their songs has been especially precious to us, and is relevant to my point here. It's called "We Have This Moment Today." The chorus reminds us that "we only have this moment to hold." We touch it briefly as it slips through our fingers like sand, and then it's gone—just another yesterday. And the problem is that tomorrow may never come, so grasp this moment now.[1]

> Being able to savor the joy of the present moment is as important as being able to recapture joy from your past.

Making the most of every moment of every day is the key to enduring happiness. Every day is filled with opportunities from which you can seize joy. True joy cannot be forced. It springs from the hearts of those who are content, grateful, and at peace with themselves, with others, and with God. Though trials and tribulations are a part of every life, making the most of any joyful moment is a habit you can develop, cultivate, and then practice on a daily basis. So make a habit of the following:

* Savor that unexpected airplane upgrade to first class they offered you when you checked in at the airport.

* Relish the time you get to spend alone when your family has gone away for the day.

* Appreciate the kind deed that your neighbor performed as a surprise.

* Squeeze out of every bad thing that happens as much good as you can.

* Squeeze out of every good thing that happens all the joy that is possible.

Keep in mind that the key to turning a behavior into a habit is to practice the action over and over again until it becomes a habit. When you begin to practice the habit of savoring the moment, it may feel awkward, even phony, at first. Yet as you continue to practice it, you will begin to feel more comfortable until it becomes a habit.

10

STEP 3—CONTROL
YOUR ADRENALINE

Be not hurried away by excitement, but say,
"Semblance, wait for me a little.
Let me see what you are and what you represent.
Let me try you."

—EPICTETUS

T urn off your pagers. Turn off your cell phones. Turn off your PDA, GameBoy, PSP, BlackBerry, iPod, and portable DVD players. It's time for you to shut down all sources of excitement, if only for the duration of this chapter. This will allow you to, as Epictetus says above, "See what they are and what they represent."

Of course, I can tell you right now what these gadgets are: they reinforce the unrelenting pursuit of excitement and constant stimulation of your adrenal system, and in the course of time, they mess up your pleasure system. I guarantee that if you do turn off these gadgets—at least while you read this chapter—you will benefit more from what I have to say than if you don't. And, who knows, you might even discover that they are not the most helpful or effective sources of pleasure.

All off? OK, then let's proceed.

THE UNIVERSAL QUEST FOR EXCITEMENT

The persistent quest for excitement is a distinguishing characteristic of modern life. And while this thrill hunt has been around for a long time (I have no doubt that primitive men got a kick out of hunting lions and tigers), during the past five years, our pursuit of extraordinary excitement has climbed to unprecedented levels. We have made excitement cheap and transportable. We can now carry our pleasure-stimulating gadgets with us wherever we go—to school, on airplanes, and in every room of our homes. They accompany us while we exercise or just take a walk through the park. Instead of walking the dog, we walk our MP3 players.

The younger you are, the greater the likelihood that you are addicted to these stimulating gadgets. But be warned: they will not only rob you of your capacity to experience pleasure in the little things of your life, but such persistent exhilaration can push your adrenal system into over-drive—with devastating consequences to your brain (depression and anxiety) and your heart (early cardiovascular disease) as we will see.

BUT ISN'T EXCITEMENT GOOD FOR US?

Already I can hear the protests. They follow me at every seminar I teach on this topic. You may be saying to yourself something like this: *But doesn't the human brain need a certain amount of stimulation to keep it functioning at its peak performance?* And here's one I often hear: "If I cut out all stimulation from my life, I'll die of boredom!" Well, I have not yet seen a corpse whose demise was caused by an overdose of tedium. Trust me, boredom does not kill. In fact, these days monotony may even help you to live longer.

But to offer a serious response to such concerns, let me say that, yes, a modicum of exhilaration aids our healthy functioning. For one, elevated exhilaration provides a form of distraction. When we go to a basketball game after a stressful day at work and cheer for our team, stressful thoughts that would otherwise obsess us are forgotten. Who cares about a nagging boss when our favorite team is winning? High spirits can also help us battle depression by stimulating our adrenaline system, which is usually turned off by depression. We know that a regular bout of exercise can help speed recovery from depression. Yes, a modicum of stimulation is good for us.

> Trust me, boredom does not kill. In fact, these days monotony may even help you to live longer.

But notice my use of the word *modicum*. These days most of us don't limit activities that are exhilarating. The more we get, the more we want. Our desire for excitement has become an addiction, and as in all addictions, our brain adapts to the present level of stimulation, gets bored with it, and then looks for more . . . and more . . . and more!

The bottom line is that our brain was not designed to enjoy a constant, high level of stimulation. It prefers lesser stimulations, preferably those that vary—a little bit up, then a little bit down. If excitement goes up and remains high constantly, the brain acclimatizes and then needs a higher level of stimulation to satisfy the now-numbed pleasure center. Clearly, when it comes to exciting pleasure, more often than not, less is better than more.

Judging by how people pursue exhilarating pleasure today, the modern mind clearly doesn't want to believe this. Aided and abetted by the media and technology, we have become sensation seekers, constantly on the lookout for the next best way to boost our feelings of well-being. Just five minutes with a TV remote control to surf your favorite cable provider will make my point. From NASCAR races to professional wrestling, from reality survival shows to the scariest places on earth, we are constantly bombarded with supplementary sensation—sensation that does not come from ordinary living but from a fantasy world. And why do we watch these shows? Because pleasure boosters like these help many get through another dull day.

> Our brain was not designed to enjoy a constant, high level of stimulation.

THE HAZARDS OF SENSATION SEEKING

The excessive pursuit of excitement, also known as *sensation seeking*, has been well studied by behavioral scientists. For starters, sensation seeking is a major cause of damaging stress. It dramatically elevates the level of circulating adrenaline and cortisol, the two major stress hormones that are primarily intended to help us deal with emergencies. The problem is, our lifestyles have become one protracted emergency. And the chronic elevation of these emergency hormones leads to high cholesterol, heart disease, depression, anxiety (especially panic anxiety disorder), and, yes, anhedonia.

But the damage goes much further. Sensation seeking is also related to a variety of sexual perversions, the use of illegal drugs (experimentation with drugs in the quest for that higher fix), unhealthy food preferences (that can cause obesity and other health problems), and risky behaviors (such as dangerous or extreme sports that provide an adrenaline rush).

MEASURING YOUR SENSATION SEEKING TENDENCY

Is your heart racing and your chest pounding? Can you feel a rush of adrenaline even as you read about sensation seeking? If you don't know whether you are a sensation seeker, then see how you score after taking the following test:

THE SENSATION-SEEKING SCALE

Definition

Sensation seeking refers to the tendency to persistently seek out activities that are invigorating, exciting, and provide a sense of adventure.

Instructions

Use the following scale to enter a score for each question:

0 = Never or rarely

1 = Occasionally

2 = Often

3 = All the time

	Score
1. I have a strong drive to get the most out of life.	_____
2. I tend to sleep fewer than seven hours a night.	_____
3. I enjoy sporting events that are very exciting.	_____
4. I prefer music that is upbeat.	_____

5. I prefer traveling to new and exotic places. _____

6. I don't avoid situations just because they are risky or dangerous. _____

7. I am adventurous and like to try new things. _____

8. I like to dress differently than other people. _____

9. I try to find fun and stimulation in what I do. _____

10. I avoid resting because I feel uncomfortable or restless. _____

11. I feel down and irritable at the start of the workweek. _____

12. Movies that don't have a lot of adventure or thrills bore me. _____

13. I get restless when I have to stay at home for any length of time. _____

14. I would like to hang-glide or take a parachute jump. _____

15. I prefer to hang out with people who are excitingly unpredictable. _____

16. When in a new restaurant, I prefer to eat food I have never eaten before. _____

17. I have sometimes hurt others when having fun at their expense. _____

18. I am game to try anything new and exciting. _____

19. When I am having fun, I ignore the negative effects of what I am doing. _____

20. When I am feeling low, I want to go out and buy things. _____

Total _____

Scoring and Interpretation

Total the score given to each question. The highest possible score is 60.

0 to 15: Your sensation-seeking tendency is extraordinarily low.

16 to 22: Your sensation-seeking tendency is low to moderate.

23 to 30: Your sensation-seeking tendency is moderate to high.

Over 30: Your sensation-seeking tendency is very high.

(Note: If your score is over 23, you may want to consider getting some professional help for your problem.)

STRATEGIES FOR CONTROLLING
YOUR ADRENALINE

A high level of sensation seeking demonstrates that you are an adrenaline junkie—you survive by extracting all the excitement you can from life. And this dependency will inevitably lead to anhedonia. Now that you have an indication of just how dependent you are on sensation seeking, let's look more closely at some of the ways you can bring this under control.

Since the excessive production of the body's stress hormones—adrenaline particularly—can significantly disrupt your pleasure system, strategies for lowering your stress are central to your emotional and pleasure health. Frankly, there is nothing more important to your life than getting *all* forms of stress—whether it comes from the good or bad things of your life—under control. You can never lower your stress level too much.

> You can never lower your stress level too much.

Here are the key steps toward developing your skills in managing your adrenaline.

Change Your Attitude About High Stimulation

I want to start here because unless you are absolutely convinced that your adrenaline dependency needs to be brought under voluntary control, you are not going to change one iota. Obviously, I don't mean that you must eliminate all sources of exhilarating stimulation; just learn to keep it within limits. Think of it as setting up speed bumps to force you to slow down.

Now I can hear my grandchildren's protests—loud, and from all nine of them. Their most favorite expression? "You only live once!" I used to say it also when I was a teenager, but what I meant was: "You should make wise choices and not waste your life on trivia. After all, you only live once!" Now it means: "Get as much excitement as you can out of life. You never know when you're gonna die!" I think my interpretation was better.

So work hard at convincing yourself that you need to lower stress in your life, and then you will be ready for the next step.

Lower Your Adrenaline

The next step is to find ways you can conserve your use of adrenaline. I use the term *conserve* intentionally. You cannot shut off adrenaline entirely. People who have deficiencies in adrenaline would die without getting regular shots of it. Effective stress management is about keeping your dependence on high, thrill-making adrenaline to a minimum.

To lower your adrenaline level, you must start by paying attention to when and where your adrenaline kicks into high gear. In my book *The Hidden Link Between Adrenaline and Stress*, I describe how you can use *stress dots* to alert you to elevated adrenaline.[2] But you don't have to use any gimmick. It's possible to tell when you are on a high simply by placing your hand on your face and seeing which is colder—assuming that you are not outdoors in a blizzard, of course, when this test would not be valid. If your hand is colder than your face, chances are that you are in high-adrenaline mode and your stress is elevated. This is because whenever your stress level goes up, adrenaline causes the arteries in your hands and feet to constrict, reducing the amount of blood present. Result? Your hands get colder. This is nature's way of preventing bleeding should you cut yourself while fleeing or fighting.

Relaxation is an important tool for lowering stress—so important that I have devoted a full chapter to the topic later in this book. In addition, the following steps will also help you to lower your adrenaline level.

* Force yourself to deliberately slow down whenever you feel rushed—even to abandon what you are doing if it really isn't that important. Very few things in life are so important that you have to do them right now.

* Try to plan ahead for periods of high demand. Emergencies do happen, but adrenaline is designed to deal with emergencies. Lack of adequate planning creates pseudoemergencies that could have been avoided. Make lists. Jot down reminders. Whatever it takes, plan ahead.

* Try not to invest life events with too much importance. It's amazing how more efficient we can become if we approach life events without catastrophizing them.

* If you feel angry or upset, get rid of your anger as soon as possible. Negative emotions such as anger or frustration are adrenaline boosters and time bombs.

* Develop skills that are needed to resolve conflicts quickly (patience, good communication skills, and a tolerance for delays) so that you can lower your frustration level.

* Develop skills that can help you get over anger as soon as possible (find out what is angering you, choose to forgive, and practice effective assertiveness skills). The Bible tells us that we should settle our anger before the sun sets (Eph. 4:26). Not a bad idea, quite frankly.

* Try to hang out with nonangry people. If your best friend is an angry person, you will likely become angry as well because anger is contagious. Friends who are low in anger are good models to follow.

* Be prepared to respond positively to criticism. This is important because all of us should be prepared to receive negative feed-back—most of which is true. The mark of a mature person is that you know this and can use negative feedback to your benefit by making appropriate changes.

* Dump the idea that anger is good for you. It isn't. Anger may feel good for a while because it gives you an adrenaline rush, but like a boomerang, it comes back and hurts you.

* Learn healthy assertiveness. Don't let others walk over you or get away with some injustice. However, remember that assertiveness is *not* aggressiveness. If you stand up for yourself only when you get angry, you are aggressive, not assertive.

* Always plan for some recovery time for your adrenal system after a period of intense arousal. Rest for your adrenal system is as important as it is for any other part of the body, so remember to always follow a period of high adrenaline demand with some down time. This is good adrenaline management.

Develop the Habit of Slowing Down

The key to stress and adrenaline management ultimately lies in developing the ability to slow down. Most of us are so absorbed with getting things done that our lives are consumed with this obsession. And there is no doubt that trying to do everything feels good. If it didn't, we would have stopped a long time ago. And when someone comments on our industriousness, especially our boss, we feel even better, forgetting that it makes everything else in our lives feel lousy.

> The key to stress and adrenaline management ultimately lies in developing the ability to slow down.

Now I know what it feels like to strive to achieve something. I am as guilty as anyone. But having a passion to make your mark and leave a lasting legacy is not the problem. Passions, dreams, and ambition are necessary in a meaningful life. But in themselves they are not the problem. It's when they become an obsession that they destroy you rather than help you build a meaningful life. When your passions begin to control you, you up the ante on anhedonia in all the other areas of your life.

The obvious solution is to try to create some balance in your work and personal life—more importantly, to learn how to slow down, even move to the slow lane if your work is destroying your happiness.

How can we develop the habit of slowing down? Here are some strategies I have personally used to get out of the fast lane:

* You must make a serious commitment to changing your lifestyle. It helps to have a companion on the way, so invite a friend in the same predicament to pact with you, and then hold each other accountable.

* Make a plan to slow down. Change isn't going to happen by accident, so make a list of your priorities, highlight what you can drop, and make a strategy to change or modify your life. Be ruthless. I regularly encounter patients whose priorities are so scrambled you could make an omelet out of them. Try to get your priorities sorted out. If there is something in your life that is really unnecessary, drop it.

* Add meaningful activities to your life. Slowing down and getting your adrenaline under control is not just about cutting out frivolous or unnecessary things. It's also about adding things that are important. It's an expensive mistake to cut out some things and then fill them with other frivolous things that are just as demanding.

Take Baby Steps Toward Stress Reduction

Stress reduction doesn't always have to involve complicated or time-consuming strategies. Here are some simple, daily activities that can also provide a strong antistress base for you life:

* Take long baths or showers. I do this often, as does my wife. She adds candles for ambience, though I prefer plain, simple darkness.

* Stroke the dog or cat. When I first heard the idea that petting a cat or dog could be profoundly relaxing, I thought the researchers were overstating their case. But then I tried it and discovered they were right.

* Listen to soothing music. Given the incredible quality of music available on MP3 players these days, a rich and portable source

of soothing music is readily available to all. You can take a player anywhere—traveling, walking, or just plain sitting on the front porch.

* Watch a sunset, or get up early and watch a sunrise. It may not be spectacular every day, but you should be able to extract some pleasure from every sunrise or sunset if your pleasure system is healthy. Just knowing that you have the gift of another day to enjoy should be enough to make you happy.

* Go for walks. I also do this with my puppy these days. We both need the exercise, so it motivates me to take a walk no matter what the weather. Unfortunately, we do not have a park nearby, so I have to settle for exploring the neighborhood. The bonus is that I am getting to know the neighbors down the road.

* Congratulate yourself on what you did right today. We don't celebrate within ourselves enough. This is a pity, because we lose an opportunity to reinforce within our brain the right sort of behaviors. The Bible talks a lot about rejoicing. We are told to "rejoice in the Lord always" (Phil. 4:4), to rejoice in our wives (Prov. 5:18), and to even to rejoice in our troubles (James 1:2). *Rejoicing* literally means *to express great joy*—and it has great therapeutic value.

START SIMPLE, BE PERSISTENT

If you want to recover your pleasure center and experience the joy of little things, it is important to control your adrenaline through the strategies outlined in this chapter. You might find it a little overwhelming and may even feel that it is more trouble than it is worth. So let me hasten to make two points before we continue to the next chapter. First, in lowering your stress, and hence your adrenaline arousal, try to focus on those areas that you feel are relevant to your life. Start with a simple exercise that you can master, then try to keep doing it until it becomes a permanent habit. Then move on to the next exercise that appeals to you. Second, remember the adage: "No pain, no gain." This is as true with the mental exercises

> Stress reduction doesn't always have to involve complicated or time-consuming strategies.

outlined in this chapter as it is for any physical exercise program. As in achieving all the good things of life, the keys to success are persistence, practice, and then perfection.

11

STEP 4—USE HUMOR TO ENHANCE YOUR HAPPINESS

Mirth is like a flash of lightning
that breaks through a gloom of clouds,
and glitters for a moment;
cheerfulness keeps up a kind of daylight in the mind,
and fills it with a steady and perpetual serenity.
—JOSEPH ADDISON, SPECTATOR. NO.381

A man walks into the vet's office with a duck on a leash.
The vet asks, "Where'd you get the pig?"
The man replies, "This is not a pig; it's a duck!"
The vet says, "I was talking to the duck."

Did you laugh? Not much? Not even a hint of a smile? Now I admit this is more of a male joke and may not be as appreciated by the ladies, but surely you were able to see some humor in the joke. If not, you really need this chapter.

Just before sitting down to write this chapter, I found the latest edition of the journal of the American Psychological Association, *Monitor on Psychology*, in my mail. The photograph on the cover caught my attention. It was relevant to the task before me. The picture was of several happy schoolchildren, mouths wide open with laughter. It was obviously a candid photograph—there's no way you can pose such joyful faces, and the laughter was too real. The caption? "Funny, but more; humor reveals the unspoken and excites the mind."

Finally, psychologists are beginning to take humor seriously. The joke I told at the beginning of this chapter was cited as one of many being used in a recent humor research, so apparently the scientists thought that it was funny enough to include in some serious research.

I was surprised to learn how much attention humor is getting these days from psychologists. As with the topic of happiness, early psychologists didn't take humor seriously. They certainly didn't see any connection between happiness and humor. But humor is now serious business. What it takes to make people laugh, and the benefits that can be derived from a good chuckle, are getting a lot of attention these days.

The psychological and medical connections between humor, happiness, and health are a major priority in research. Hospitals are now using laughter therapy groups for patients with chronic pain. A notice that appeared recently on a hospital's bulletin board sums up the idea by exhorting, "Jest for the health of it."

LAUGHTER HEALS THE BODY AND MIND

Laughter is a great healing force to both the body and the mind. For instance, it maximizes the body's ability to heal itself. Pleasurable laughter facilitates the body's immune system, making healing easier. But it also facilitates emotional immunity and our spiritual growth.

So why don't we laugh more? Possibly because we have become anhedonic.

Not long ago, a newspaper reporter visited a retreat conducted by a prominent physician who specializes in the treatment of terminally ill cancer patients. He talked with a large number of cancer victims ranging in age from seventeen to seventy. All had been diagnosed as terminal and been given last-resort treatments. Now they were gathered at this retreat to learn how to live their last months to the fullest.

What impressed the reporter most about this retreat was the laughter. According to her, the air was full of it. After ten days of sharing and facing the reality of their circumstances, the cancer sufferers had come to the point that they could laugh freely with each other—a shared communion of mirth. They were funny and fun-loving, and their humor moved the newspaper reporter deeply. Some told her that

---

❋

SOME FACTS ABOUT HUMOR

- While children laugh about three hundred times a day, adults laugh only fifteen times a day.
- Laughter is a complex phenomenon. Now that psychologists are finally paying attention to it, more than one hundred theories about humor have emerged in recent times.
- Laughter has beneficial effects. As Mark Twain said, "When you laugh, your mind, body, and spirit change."
- Even the most troubled marriages can benefit from the introduction of humor into the relationship. Humorous couples seldom divorce.
- When people laugh together, they feel more bonded and can survive tough times more easily.
- Being able to laugh at yourself builds self-acceptance and lowers stress significantly.

when they had been in the best of health, they had never learned really to laugh at themselves and their problems. Now they could do this with great feeling. And with this new freedom to laugh came a new depth to their lives.

And what was the health result? Of course, humor by itself doesn't cure cancer. But the physician conducting the retreat reported that many of the cancer patients attending these last-resort retreats outlive their short life expectancies. Their immune systems become stimulated by the pleasure their laughter encouraged, and they achieve a new perspective on life. The progress of their disease is slowed and, in a few cases, possibly reversed.

> So why don't we laugh more? Possibly because we have become anhedonic.

There can be no doubt that our minds and bodies do indeed respond to a happy environment, especially to a happy internal environment.

IT IS A LAUGHING MATTER

Not only did the APA article get my attention, but as I looked through the rest of my mail I noticed an advertisement from a prominent psychologist who regularly offers continuing education seminars. Psychologists, like many professional groups, are required to continue our education in order to stay licensed. And would you believe it, the advertisement for the seminar from this prominent psychologist was on the use of humor in psychotherapy. This was a first. Not only are psychologists waking up to the importance of humor, but we're becoming a bit obsessive about it. It's a good obsession, however.

We have known for a long time that humor—more specifically, a long, deep belly laugh—has enormous health benefits. Blood pressure goes down, stress dissipates, anger subsides, the immune system kicks in extra disease-fighting killer cells, oxygen circulation increases, and the brain becomes more active. It seems that there is nothing that laughter isn't good for. Even your personality can undergo a major makeover if you learn to laugh more.

And then I had a good chuckle. Why? Well, until recently psychotherapy was considered to be a serious endeavor. You never joked about it.

I clearly remember an incident in my early training. I was discussing a case of severe depression with my supervisor. In passing, I mentioned that at one point in the therapy I had made a humorous

> Our minds and bodies do indeed respond to a happy environment, especially to a happy internal environment.

comment, and my patient actually laughed—the first time in more than four months. My supervisor raked me over the coals. Even though my patient had told me as he was leaving the session that it felt good to be able to laugh again, my supervisor chastised me for interjecting a humorous comment during my psychotherapy. "Psychotherapy," she rebuked, "is serious business, and you must not minimize it or do anything to distract from the therapeutic process." What? Helping someone who is depressed have a good laugh has no therapeutic value? You've got to be kidding.

Deep down, I disagreed. I couldn't care what the psychotherapy gurus believed; for me humor is, and always has been, therapeutic.

LAUGHTER AND EMOTIONAL HEALTH

The health benefits of laughter have been known throughout history. Even the Bible mentions it: "A cheerful heart is good medicine" is an oft-quoted proverb (Prov. 17:22). But it is not only physical health that is enhanced by it. Emotional health is also dependent on it, psychologists are now acknowledging. And it is this benefit of laughter and humor that I want to address here because it plays a vital role in both protecting and restoring our pleasure center. (I sure hope that supervisor from my early training is reading this right now.)

And this brings me to a very important point. Healthy humor can only occur if your pleasure system is working properly. In other words, like happiness, humor depends on the pleasure system to add the sense of enjoyment to what is funny. Anhedonic people are not able to experience any pleasure in humor.

> Anhedonic people are not able to experience any pleasure in humor.

Test it for yourself. The next time you are with someone who is depressed, try making a humorous comment and watch his face. There will be no smile. When your pleasure system is not functioning normally, even the funniest of jokes cannot be appreciated. Because anhedonia is the central symptom in serious depression, the depressed person cannot enjoy anything, especially in the early stages of depression, and this includes humor. You only begin to see laughter return, as in the case of the patient I referred to earlier, when the depression is starting to lift. If a person can have a hearty laugh at a funny joke, that person is probably not clinically depressed.

IMPROVING YOUR LAUGHTER QUOTIENT

Just as we all have an intelligence quotient (IQ) and an emotional quotient (EQ), we also have a laughter quotient (LQ)—according to laughter experts. The higher your LQ, the more you are able to appreciate healthy humor. You would make a fabulous audience for any comedian.

Notice that I said *healthy* humor. Dirty humor is not really funny at all. I am not saying this because I am a prig—far from it. Yes, an inappropriate joke gets a laugh, but it's funny only because it is dirty, not because there is real humor of any sort. The laugh comes from the shock reaction to something said or done that is normally distasteful or disgusting. So don't be surprised if this type of laughter does not offer healing to your pleasure center. If anything, it feeds your addictive process because it creates a humor response that needs some gross expression to get your pleasure center going. If you can only laugh at dirty humor, you probably have a low LQ, and it may need some recovery help.

> Improving laughter ability can bring healing to many parts of a hurting person.

So let's measure your laughter quotient (LQ).

❉
LAUGHTER QUOTIENT (LQ) SCALE

Instructions

Circle T for true or F for false for the following questions:

1. I enjoy laughing at jokes and funny stories. T / F
2. I do not find dirty humor to be very funny. T / F
3. I avoid sarcasm and negative or ethnic-based jokes or humor. T / F
4. My family and friends would say that I am a happy person and laugh a lot. T / F
5. I can laugh even when things are going badly in my life. T / F

6. I can laugh at funny jokes or cartoons even when
   I am alone.   T / F

7. Even if no one else is laughing, I have no problem
   laughing myself.   T / F

8. My sense of humor is never offensive and benefits
   my family and friends.   T / F

9. Sometimes I see humor in things that others don't.   T / F

10. I can laugh at myself when I have done something
    stupid.   T / F

Scoring and Interpretation

Of the ten questions above, how many do you answer as True?

8 or more: You have an exceptionally high LQ.

  5 to 7:   You have a high LQ.

  3 to 5:   You have a low LQ.

  0 to 3:   You have hardly anything going in the laughter
             department of your brain.

Now I am not suggesting that a high LQ can remedy a major disorder like depression, where laughter is as painful as having a tooth extracted without an anesthetic. While it might be possible to distract a depressed person from his pain occasionally, a healthy humor or laughter response can go a long way to healing normal anhedonia. There is also evidence that laughter can activate the chemistry of the will to live. People on the verge of suicide can be helped to regain a healthy perspective on life through the medicine of laughter. Put together, improving laughter ability can bring healing to many parts of a hurting person.

STIMULATING YOUR BRAIN'S LAUGHTER CENTER

It stands to reason that laughter is triggered by something in the brain. So it is no surprise that scientists have now actually located a *laughter center* in the brain. As with the discovery of the pleasure center, this discovery was quite by accident.

Scientists were exploring a sixteen-year-old girl's epilepsy, trying to find ways to cure it. Accidentally, they inserted electrodes in a part of the brain where, when they passed an electrical current through it, the girl laughed uncontrollably—and there was nothing funny going on. A low voltage got a smile, a higher voltage got a very big smile, and higher still got a raucous laugh. And here is an interesting fact: the laugh was contagious. Everyone in the operating room would burst out laughing in response to the girl's laughter. Laughter is definitely contagious. If you laugh more, those around you will laugh more also.

> If you laugh more, those around you will laugh more also.

While you do have a laughter center in your brain, you cannot go to the doctor's office and get a few laughter shocks. (Although I anticipate that a time will come when laughter will be so scarce that a form of treatment involving stimulation of the laughter center might be commonplace.) So we have to create ways for stimulating this center ourselves—natural ways, preferably. Here are several exercises that can help you stimulate your laughter center and increase your laughter quotient. In the process, you will also heal your pleasure center as well.

Exercise 1: Lighten Up and Brighten Up!
To take life, or yourself, too seriously is a laughter killer. If you are a

❋ TYPES OF HUMOR

You can improve your appreciation for humor by understanding the different types of humor and knowing what type tickles your funny bone.

Here are some of the major types of humor. Place a check mark next to the types of humor that grab you.[1]

• PLAY ON WORDS
Question: Why will you never starve in the desert? Answer: Because of the sandwiches there.

• PUNS
In the delivery room, the unborn infant expected to be given a wide berth.

• "WHAT'S WRONG WITH THIS?" HUMOR
Most home projects are impossible, which is why you should do them yourself. There is no point in paying other people to mess things up when you can easily do it yourself for far less money.

serious person by nature, then try to be aware of when and where you act this way. Even if you generally feel that you are a serious person, remember that this doesn't mean you have to behave seriously all the time. Take some time out from your seriousness and try to brighten up your life a little.

Exercise 2: Increase Your Laughter Awareness

Here are some ways you can increase your laughter awareness:

Look for humor around you. On the bus or train to work, in the classroom, walking down the street, when you are shopping, or even listening to a sermon. I heard of someone who was in the post office sending some parcels just before Christmas.

"When do you want them delivered by?" asked the clerk.

"By Christmas," replied the lady, a little peeved because it was so obvious.

Realizing her inappropriate question, the quick-witted clerk replied,

"Yes, but which Christmas?" Customer and clerk broke into laughter. If you look for humor, you'll find it all around you.

Look for humor in yourself and what you do. It's healthy to laugh at yourself. It helps to relieve guilt and speeds your self-forgiveness whenever you feel embarrassed. Since you are human, you will inevitably end up feeling oversensitive or embarrassed when you do stupid things. Dropping in a word of appropriate humor can cancel out the embarrassment and help to build friendships. People are attracted to self-accepting people.

Try improving the humor in cartoons and jokes you encounter. In

> • PARODY
> An advertisement: "Dare to be the same—Kalvin Klone Jeans"
> • SATIRE
> One revolutionary leader to his next in command: "Mira, mi hermano! Why should I give you six stars on your shoulders? Surely, four stars are enough. But six? What would you do with six stars? Swim to Miami? Fly to the moon?"
> • RIDICULE
> A common form of humor often used in politics to discredit the opposition in which you make *fun of others. It is not a healthy form of comedy. I discourage it.*

other words, take a joke or cartoon and try to make it even funnier by modifying it—removing any inappropriate content. For me, this modification is fun. I hardly repeat a joke or cartoon as delivered but try to improve it as an exercise in toning up my LQ.

Let me give you an example. The joke I started this chapter with was different in the original. You will recall that it was a joke mentioned in the APA journal article on humor that is often used in humor research. I suppose it is what you would call a standardized joke so that people's laughter responses can be measured. However, when I read the original version of the joke, it was mildly offensive. A bartender, not a vet. But what has a bar got to do with a pig or duck? It implies that you have to be a little drunk. Also, I happen to view alcoholism as a serious problem and don't laugh at drunken jokes. Besides, a vet deals with animals, not a bartender. So I made a few changes. Now go back and read the joke again and see if you agree that it is funnier my way. And if it isn't funnier for you, then try to modify it so that it is.

Avoid becoming a standup comic. Very few people have what it takes to be a successful standup comic. It is a rare gift. So whatever you do to improve your LQ, forget about turning yourself into a comedian and leave that to the professionals. Telling jokes is not what increasing your LQ is all about. The laughter has to be for you, not others, and it must come from deep within you. It's about you enjoying humor, not about trying to be funny to gain others' approval.

Daily, help someone else to laugh. You don't have to be a comedian to do this, just a friend. We all know people who can make us smile, just by being themselves. Often it's because they can laugh at how ridiculously serious we can be, or they are able to see something funny even in the most serious of life events. We enjoy having them around because they lift our spirits. Well, become such a person and you'll give your own LQ a boost.

Exercise 3: Building Your Laughter Reflex

Humor, like many mental skills, has to be developed so that it is a natural reflex. You shouldn't have to think about humor; it should be spontaneous. Train yourself to think funny. To do this, you have to create a filter in your thinking through which everything you see, hear, or touch is passed to find bits and pieces of humor. This helps to give us a brighter, more optimistic outlook. If you don't do this intentionally, you may tend to look at the pessimistic, negative side of life. It also helps you to "think funny" more than you would ordinarily do.

For instance, when you sit down to read the newspaper or watch the news, try to catch any funny, humorous things. A misprint in a newspaper advertisement or a mispronunciation by the newsreader might qualify. I heard of a notice in a church bulletin that read: "The low self-esteem support group will meet in the church hall this Thursday evening at 7 p.m. Please use the back door when you enter." Oops! Or what about the following sermon announcement: "Don't let worry kill you. Let the church help!"

> Notice how much humor there is all around you.

Catching humorous moments like this should not have a malicious intent. You are not trying to criticize or look down on other people; instead, you are merely using naturally occurring mistakes to feed your humor sensitivity. Just notice how much humor there is all around you.

Exercise 4. A Daily Laughter Workout

We give a lot of attention to exercising our bodies, but not much to exercising our minds. A daily laughter workout can tone up your LQ.

To do your LQ workout, set aside twenty or thirty minutes each day and use it to listen to a humorous CD, watch a comedy television show or movie, or read a humorous book. I combine my laughter workout with my physical workout by listening to a funny CD while I walk on my treadmill or take my dog for a walk in the neighborhood. I've listened to nearly all of Garrison Keillor's Lake Wobegon stories, Jeff Allen's comedy CDs, and a host of others. I have even copied the soundtrack of funny movies onto an MP3 player so they can travel with me as I jog. I have no shortage of humorous material at my disposal. It also has a secondary benefit in that my laughter workout is a rich source of speaking material for sermons and seminars.

If you enjoy keeping a journal, you may want to set aside a section each day so that you can focus and preserve laughter and humor in your life. This is an excellent way to capture funny moments so that you can go back and recapture happy moments later in your life. It helps to build a positive perspective.

> Humor and laughter can have a significant influence on your ability to lower stress and enhance your health.

The bottom line is that humor and laughter can have a significant influence on your ability to lower stress and enhance your health. A healthy sense of humor can help you to achieve a balance between your inner and outer self as well as your work and your play.

After all, *today is the first day of the rest of your laugh!*

STEP 5—DEVELOP APPRECIATION AND GRATITUDE

Reflect on your present blessings,
of which every man has many,
not on your misfortunes,
of which all men have some.
—CHARLES DICKENS

If it is important to maintain a healthy pleasure system that can deliver an enduring sense of happiness, then it is crucial to find out how this can be accomplished. Psychology is helping us immensely here, and the tools being developed are simple and easy to master.

In a recent experiment, psychologists asked undergraduates to complete a survey that included a happiness scale and measures of gratitude and thankfulness. Then over the next six weeks, the participants wrote down, once a week, five things for which they were grateful. It had a dramatic effect on their happiness score, and all rated themselves higher in happiness after the six weeks than before.[1] It's hard to feel envy, greed, or bitterness when you're grateful.

APPRECIATION AND GRATITUDE

Appreciation and gratitude are both powerful concepts. But the perceptive reader might well ask, "What do these have to do with the brain's pleasure system?" A good question. They have a lot more to do with your pleasure system than you might suppose. And because appreciation and gratitude have strong religious overtones, I cannot help but include some of my own Christian perspectives on these important topics. But please remember, these two topics are important whether or not you embrace any religious foundation. Everyone needs to have an enlarged capacity for appreciation and gratitude. Both help the human brain to regulate the delivery of pleasure.

> Everyone needs to have an enlarged capacity for appreciation and gratitude.

Appreciation and gratitude are emotional states of mind that both help to create the right conditions for pleasure—pleasure that is enduring and that can never become addicting. If you could become addicted to showing appreciation and gratitude, it would be an addiction worth pursuing.

These emotional states not only help us to experience pleasure in the ordinary things of life, but they also help to protect the pleasure system in the brain from being led astray and depending only on super-flooded thrills that can numb our pleasure pathways. They help to soothe and heal the pleasure system when it has been abused.

Because appreciation and gratitude can do all these wonderful things for our brains, I need to sound a warning: these exercises can bring about a drastic makeover for your life. So be aware, you continue at the risk of becoming a really happy person.

WHAT'S SO GREAT ABOUT APPRECIATION AND GRATITUDE?

Why are appreciation and gratitude so therapeutically powerful? How do they connect our thinking with our pleasure system? And is there clear scientific evidence that they can help us to build a healthy pleasure system and undo our anhedonia? I'll get to the first two questions shortly, but to the last question the answer is yes. Whereas a mere ten years ago psychologists hardly paid any attention to these concepts, today there is a flurry of activity as researchers scramble to unlock their therapeutic mysteries.

> Appreciation is the understanding of the nature or meaning of something you value.

We've known about the power of gratitude to transform our emotions for a long time. Thankfulness can be traced back more than two thousand years. It appears frequently in the Bible, where believers are admonished, "Give thanks in all circumstances, for this is God's will for you" (1 Thess. 5:18). But it is only in the past five years that psychologists have begun putting together all the pieces for gratitude and appreciation—and, I might add, being quite successful at it.

The remarkable research being undertaken in this area would take a book to describe. However, I hope that what I do present on the close cousins of appreciation and gratitude will convince you of their importance in rebuilding your pleasure system. On the way, they should also help you in your stress management and the achievement of authentic happiness.

APPRECIATION

As I have indicated, appreciation and gratitude are close cousins. It is sometimes hard to tell where one ends and the other begins, and you certainly can't have the one without the other. For the sake of learning how to enhance both of them, we first need to look at them separately.

Appreciation is the understanding of the nature or meaning of something you value. I can appreciate a beautiful sunset even though I know little about the meteorology or chemistry that creates it. The effect of the sunset is caused by dust and moisture in the air, experts tell me, but who cares when it looks so beautiful. I can also appreciate a gift someone has given me. I don't need to know how much it cost or how much of a sacrifice was made to buy or make it.

> Gratitude, then, adds a feeling of emotional indebtedness toward someone who has done something you appreciate.

Gratitude is somewhat different from appreciation in that it has more to do with people than things and with motives than facts. For instance, I can appreciate a beautiful sunset, but I hardly feel any gratitude toward it. Gratitude, then, adds a feeling of emotional indebtedness toward someone who has done something you appreciate. Also, when I realize how much time someone put in to make a gift for me, I am overwhelmed with gratitude to the giver. I can appreciate being served well by a competent store clerk, but I don't necessarily need to feel indebted (gratitude) for the service. That's what clerks are paid to do.

So when we feel gratitude, we not only feel appreciation but also have a strong desire to thank the person or to reciprocate the favor they have done for us. Gratitude means that we have added a sense of indebtedness to our appreciation. One (appreciation) is the foundation for the other (gratitude). But we need them both.

In this sense, appreciation must precede gratitude. This difference helps me because it means that I must first work at becoming more appreciative—to the world around me and to the people I encounter as I pass through this world. Then I can learn to build a more robust and persistent gratitude toward those who deserve it. And to be quite frank, a lot of us need to work at increasing our appreciation and gratitude attitudes. Our pleasure system needs it to stay healthy.

> Appreciation is also about fostering a deep inner habit of appreciating the good things in your life.

In a religious context, the term *gratitude* goes one step beyond this, so let me clarify it for my religious-oriented readers. The term *gratitude* is often used to describe a feeling of immense indebtedness toward God for what He has done for us, and often forms the basis for much of our worship practices. Worship, for many, is an expression of the gratitude for blessings bestowed upon them. So while gratitude is one step up the ladder from appreciation, spiritual gratitude is yet one further step up from human gratitiude.

PRACTICING DAILY APPRECIATION

One of the most commonly used exercises for enhancing appreciation is to make it a habit to express appreciation to someone at least once each day. It can be a word of appreciation to a shop clerk who has served you well, the postman who has just brought a parcel to your front door,

STRENGHTENING YOUR APPRECIATION

Here is an exercise you can do to strengthen your appreciation.

1. When you are feeling frazzled and overextended, take some time out. Find a quiet spot where you will not be interrupted for twenty or thirty minutes, sit comfortably, and relax. If you are a person of faith, take a moment to pray for a calming of your mind.

2. Now make a sincere effort to shift your focus away from whatever is racing in your mind or disturbing your emotions, toward the area around your heart. Visualize your heart, as if you can see it beating.

3. Try to recall a positive, fun feeling or happy time in your life and attempt to reexperience it in your imagination. Retrieve whatever feelings you had about it.

someone who works under you or above you.

I have intentionally increased my expressions of appreciation significantly in the last few years. I do it now at every opportunity—with the same result every time: I feel better for doing it. I can't explain exactly why I should be the beneficiary of saying thank you to someone else just passing through my life, but I do. I have a strong suspicion it has something to do with my pleasure center. It's as if my brain is designed to reinforce appreciation by giving an extra boost of dopamine to my pleasure center—and I feel really good.

Another very helpful way to enhance your daily appreciation is to write regular notes of appreciation whenever you can. I confess that I have not been very good at this myself, but I know many who are, including my wife.

But appreciation is not just about saying thank you and writing encouraging notes. Appreciation is also about fostering a deep inner habit of appreciating the good things in your life. In the next exercise, we will look at ways for turning appreciation into gratitude.

GRATITUDE

We now turn to the cousin of appreciation—gratitude. The so-called positive psychology revolution that I previously alluded to has made fostering gratitude a major focus of therapeutic attention. It serves as a major buffer, when regularly practiced, to many mental illnesses. It is also a major player in fostering authentic happiness.

With psychology now focused more on building strengths and finding buffers against mental illness than on just finding cures for mental illness, many research psychologists have begun to look more closely at beneficial emotional states like gratitude and optimism. You will be hearing a lot more about these emotional states in the future, as the serious research has only just begun.

4. Now just remain in a quiet state, and focus on your feelings of appreciation. Tell yourself what it is you appreciate. Who you appreciate. Why you appreciate. Try to remain in a state of appreciation for as long as you can. You can use prayer to focus on thankfulness to God, His blessings in your life, and the good things that come to you from others.

5. Listen to your heart. Feel it beat in your body. Try to sustain a calm, appreciative state as long as you can. When you are done, slowly restart your life and try to maintain the appreciative feeling through the rest of the day.

A good time to do this exercise is when you are trying to fall asleep. Instead of reaching for a sleeping pill or counting sheep, try putting yourself to sleep with this appreciation exercise. The ability to create and maintain an attitude or state of appreciation is a powerful de-stressor.

THE VALUE OF A GRATITUDE ATTITUDE

That gratitude is a powerful healer has been demonstrated by several studies using *gratitude interventions*. Here are some examples that can help to convince you of the value of maintaining a consistent feeling of gratitude.

In one university study, people suffering from a painful neuro-muscular disorder were instructed to regularly keep a record of things they could be grateful for. A kind word from someone. A gift from a neighbor. The smell of orange blossoms in the spring. Life is full of little things to be grateful for, and these sufferers learned how to count their blessings. The results were astonishing. Improving in their pain management, they felt happier and emotionally more stable.

In an experimental comparison, those who kept gratitude journals on a weekly basis exercised more regularly, reported fewer physical symptoms, felt better about their lives as a whole, and were more optimistic about the upcoming week, compared to those who recorded hassles or neutral life events.

> This is the secret to building your gratitude attitude: remind yourself often about things you need to be grateful for.

A daily gratitude intervention of self-guided exercises with young adults resulted in higher reported levels of the positive states of alertness, enthusiasm, determination, attentiveness, and energy compared to a focus on hassles or a downward social comparison (ways in which participants thought they were better off than others). There was no difference in levels of unpleasant emotions reported in the three groups.

So whereas gratitude was once the forgotten factor in happiness research, it has now reclaimed its prestigious position.

PRACTICE MAKES PERFECT

That gratefulness can be improved by practice is beyond dispute. But where do beginners begin or backsliders get back on track?

The first and obvious starting point is to pay attention to what is going on around you. Reverse your neglect of this important virtue, and you will find that you can grow the seeds of gratefulness just by making room for them. Pay more attention to the many blessings that come your way every day. Research has shown that by noticing and appreciating the good elements in your life, you can improve your general outlook and well-being. And this is the secret to building your gratitude attitude: remind yourself often about things you need to be grateful for.

The second key is to find a way to express your gratitude. It is not enough to just think it or even just to feel it; you must share it with another. Unlike just thinking about your gratitude, speaking about it helps to reinforce the gratitude in your brain and sends it far and wide throughout your nervous system.

Of course there will be times when it will not be easy to find anything to be grateful about. In times of despair, many have turned to the Bible to help them discover a key to gratitude. At times when I find it difficult to be grateful, I turn to verses like Psalm 31:7. In this psalm, King David feels utterly abandoned. Everyone has turned against him. He is utterly distressed. Then he turns to God and says, "I will be glad and rejoice in your love, for you saw my affliction and knew the anguish of my soul." Down the centuries, many have found solace through such expressions of gratitude toward God.

GRATITUDE EXERCISES

Now let's consider a few ways we can learn to enhance our feelings of gratitude. There are three exercises I would like to present here: the Glad Game, the Gratitude Game, and the "I Wish You Enough" Game.

The Glad Game

Gladness is a feeling, and sometimes it comes wrapped with gratitude. However, you have to learn to be glad before you can feel gratitude. If you don't know how to turn on your gladness, you're not going to be effective in turning on gratitude. However, the border between gladness and gratitude is not always very clear.

Many readers will immediately recognize this game. You'll find it described in that delightful novel *Pollyanna*, written in 1913 by Eleanor H. Porter. The book became a children's classic though I suspect it has had a greater impact on adults than children. It has certainly taught me a lot.

Pollyanna tells the story of a young girl who is adopted after her father's death by her very wealthy but disillusioned, grumpy, and unhappy Aunt Polly. The wealthy Miss Polly is less than pleased at the thought of having to take in a child to live in her home, but since she is the eleven-year-old's only living relative, she has no choice.

Through Pollyanna's influence, the grumpy, dissatisfied inhabitants of the town become miraculously pleasant. She transforms them by teaching them the Glad Game, a game her father taught her about finding a silver lining in every cloud. With only Aunt Polly to care for her and a harsh daily regimen of study and no play, Pollyanna has to rely on her Glad Game more and more to survive.

The first night with her aunt, Pollyanna is punished for coming late to dinner and sent to the kitchen with just bread and milk. Her aunt's maid, Nancy, tries to comfort her.

"I'm sorry about the bread and milk; I am; I am."

"Oh, I'm not. I'm glad," replies Pollyanna.

"Glad! Why?"

"Why, I like bread and milk, and I'd like to eat with you. I don't see any trouble about being glad about that."

Pollyanna then goes on to explain the game her father had taught her. She had played it ever since she was a young girl. Always find something to be glad about, no matter how terrible things feel. And Pollyanna demonstrates again and again that you can always find something to be glad about.

I encourage you to read the story for yourself. Pay attention to how the Glad Game transforms the life not only of a little girl but also of an entire town.

The rules for the Glad Game are simple. Every time something bad happens in your life, instead of wallowing in your misery, find something redeeming in your circumstances, and then focus your thoughts on what is good about it. Pollyanna once received a Christmas gift of crutches from the Ladies Aid society—they didn't have any more dolls. So what can you be glad about if you receive a Christmas gift of a couple of old crutches that nobody wants? "Just be glad you don't need them," she says. Every cloud has a silver lining. Find it and then hang on for dear life.

What do you have to be glad about today? Got the Monday morning blues? Well, be glad because you woke up this morning. Be glad for the bed you slept in and the roof over your head. Many do not have either. Be glad for your health and be glad because you have enough to eat each day. Encourage yourself to feel gladness for the people who care about you and love you unconditionally.

True, there are some things so bad all you can do is grieve over them. Pollyanna acknowledged this—and since she's the expert in the Glad Game, she should know. "It's harder," she says, "and sometimes it's too hard—like when your father goes to heaven, and there isn't anybody . . . left."

I used the Glad Game myself a couple of years ago in order to open up my gratitude for what I experienced. Out of the blue, I found myself confronted with the discovery that I had five blockages in my heart arteries and needed emergency heart surgery. My schedule was full. In a week I was due to go to Korea to speak at a conference. It was most upsetting—and downright inconvenient. Why did it have to come now? I was frustrated and anxious over the outcome of the surgery.

Then I remembered the Glad Game. So I asked myself what there was in this situation I could be glad about. What redeeming feature could I find in this devastating discovery—something that could shift my misery to something I could be glad about?

It took only a moment, and I had gladness all over me. Because my family on my father's side is riddled with heart disease, I had always feared that I would be struck with a heart attack. And here I was, not having had a heart attack (which makes for a better prognosis) and being offered surgery that would give me a whole new lease on life. So what did I choose? Misery at having to cancel out on all my activities or gladness because my life has been spared? You guess. It opened the door to the gratitude I should have felt about my life being saved before I had a heart attack.

The Gratitude Game

The Gratitude Game—closely related to the Glad Game—is different in several respects in psychological circles. Psychologists consider gratitude to be a more mature emotion than gladness, but I strongly believe that you cannot capture gratitude if you cannot create gladness. How does it differ from the gladness? Gratitude is an attitude of thankfulness for anything that should be appreciated. Gladness is the experience of joy or happiness that should accompany gratitude—but doesn't always. To illustrate, I was certainly most grateful for the discovery of my blocked arteries before I had a heart attack, but I wasn't exactly glad about it. You really have to work at being both grateful and glad. In some rare circumstances, I suppose one should settle for gratitude even when there is nothing to be glad about.

> Every few days, but no longer apart than once a week, take a few minutes to record events or people in your life you are grateful for.

In the Gratitude Game, you endeavor to find whatever it is in your life you can be grateful for—even though you might not exactly be glad about it. Just focus on gratitude.

Many exercises on how to enhance your gratitude have recently appeared on the Internet. Here is my variation of Dr. Seligman's original Gratitude Game.[1] You need to have either a small notebook or a few index cards that you can carry with you. In this exercise, it is important that you actually write down your answers. Doing this reinforces your gratitude and helps you to remember it longer.

Every few days, but no longer apart than once a week, take a few minutes to record events or people in your life you are grateful for.

* Recall any acts of love or kindness directed toward you in the past few days. These acts of love or kindness may have been done by friends, family, or strangers. Recall how you felt at the time. Perhaps it was someone offering you his seat on the bus or

someone allowing you to go ahead of her in line. Make a brief note identifying each gratitude.

* Recall events from your past that now you are grateful for, acts of love and kindness or emotional issues that served you within the last few weeks, months, or years. Perhaps it was a word of wisdom from your father or a friend. Perhaps a kind deed done to you as a child that you have never forgotten. Note them and allow yourself to feel your gratitude and appreciation.

* Recall all the wonderful people who love and care for you. Make a list of all their names, then alongside each name, list three special things about that person.

Then whenever you feel disappointed or down, or if you are overcome with a desire to review the many things you are grateful for in your life, pull out your notebook or cards and remind yourself that you are a very fortunate person to have so many things to be thankful for.

The "I Wish You Enough" Game

To add to the Glad and Gratitude Games, I came across this game recently. It can significantly boost your gratitude by helping you to adopt an attitude of contentment in your life, not unlike what the apostle Paul advocates in Philippians 4:11: "I have learned to be content whatever the circumstances."

A little story by an unknown author, "What Is Enough?" came in my e-mail the other day from a friend. I hope it strikes a chord with you the way it did with me. The story goes something like this:

Recently I overheard a mother and daughter in their last moments together at the airport. They had announced the departure. Standing near the security gate, they hugged and the mother said, "I love you and I wish you enough."

The daughter replied, "Mom, our life together has been more than enough. Your love is all I ever needed. I wish you enough, too, Mom."

They kissed and the daughter left. The mother walked over to the window where I was seated. Standing there, I could see she wanted and needed to cry. I tried not to intrude on her privacy, but she welcomed me in by asking, "Did you ever say good-bye to someone, knowing it would be forever?"

"Yes, I have," I replied. "Forgive me for asking, but why is this a 'forever' good-bye?"

"I am old, and she lives so far away. I have challenges ahead, and the reality is—the next trip back will be for my funeral," she said.

"When you were saying good-bye, I heard you say, 'I wish you enough.' May I ask what that means?"

She began to smile. "That's a wish that has been handed down from other generations. My parents used to say it to everyone."

She paused a moment and looked up as if trying to remember it in detail. "When we said, 'I wish you enough' we were wanting the other person to have a life filled with just enough good things to sustain them." Then turning toward me she shared the following, as if she were reciting it from memory:

"I wish you enough sun to keep your attitude bright.

I wish you enough rain to appreciate the sun more.

I wish you enough happiness to keep your spirit alive.

I wish you enough pain so that the smallest joys in life appear much bigger.

I wish you enough gain to satisfy your wanting.

I wish you enough loss to appreciate all that you possess.

I wish you enough hellos to get you through the final good-bye."

What a powerful message. Most of us have more than enough in our lives yet cannot appreciate what is really important. We just don't realize that the *more than enough* keeps us from appreciating what is significant. So try to be mindful of the everyday things we most take for granted, such as our health, friends, and family. Be content with what you have, and gratitude will flow more freely. With more than enough, is it any wonder that we cannot find real, abiding pleasure anymore? The more we have, the further we drive our pleasure system away from it.

> Most of us have more than enough in our lives, yet cannot appreciate what is really important.

I close with this simple message to all my readers, friends, and loved ones: I wish you enough. No more and no less.

STEP 6—MASTER RELAXATION AND MEDITATION

Summing it all up, friends, I'd say you'll do best
by filling your minds
and meditating on things true, noble,
reputable, authentic, compelling, gracious—
the best, not the worst; the beautiful, not the ugly;
things to praise, not things to curse.
—THE APOSTLE PAUL (PHIL. 4:8 MSG)

Got a minute? Probably not, so I'll make this quick. A recent poll shows that Americans are about the most impatient people on God's earth.[1] And we get antsy whenever we have to wait. Whether someone puts you on hold for five minutes on the phone or you have to stand in line for fifteen minutes at the supermarket, waiting drives most people up the wall. Frankly, it drives me crazy too.

But our low tolerance for waiting goes much deeper than this. Bottom line is that our nerves are frayed. We live on the edge for most of the day and then have an emotional blowup whenever we are forced to stop. And it doesn't take much to push us off the ledge of patient endurance. We are all too distracted, busy, and stressed out for our own good. We are bombarded with words, media images, and social demands at a pace that is beyond what we were created for.

PATIENCE IS A VIRTUE—OR IS IT?

Now, what's this all got to do with our pleasure center? It is because we are slowly losing our capacity to tolerate a moment of quiet motionlessness. Anhedonia makes us impatient and irritable. It blocks our awareness and enjoyment of God, dampens spiritual inspiration and the necessary pathways for character transformation. If we can't wait patiently in line at the grocery store, it's hard to "wait on the Lord" and enjoy His still, quiet presence. This is why it is essential to break the yoke of unfocused, busy, overextended living.

> We are slowly losing our capacity to tolerate a moment of quiet motionlessness.

Learning to calm the body and mind through relaxation and experiencing quiet patience through spiritual practices can reverse this dilemma. They are essential to our health and well-being. Then instead of waiting and turbulent times being stressful, you can draw on relaxation and meditation techniques to make them more tolerable.

Relaxation and meditation run counter to our busy culture. We are used to speed-reading, sound bites, first impressions, and skimming. Unfortunately, that is as deep as we often want to go, and we suffer the depleting consequences. Relaxation provides an opportunity for the body and mind to calm down, and the often-neglected spiritual discipline of contemplative meditation provides our souls and bodies a reprieve from the noisy, busy, fast-paced culture. Prayer and meditation turn us from the constant noise around us to intentional times of silence, from the busyness of life to solitude, and from running fast to slowing down to pay attention to what matters most.

THE SCIENTIFIC VALIDATION OF RELAXATION

The power of simple relaxation exercises has been validated for many years. The word *rest* occurs again and again in Scripture. In the early nineteenth century and prior, something called the *second sleep* was highly valued. Second sleep, also called *beauty sleep* in a time when people went to bed early, refers to the early hours of the morning when one usually sleeps much more lightly. During a period of wakefulness before the second sleep, people would meditate, and take in the good, quiet things of life. Usually lasting about an hour, this was a time of day that was highly prized.

Then we invented the electric light and prolonged the daytime. People went to bed later and so-called second sleep became history. People go to bed so late now that they don't get enough sleep in general, let alone have the luxury of some beauty sleep.

So what needs to take its place? One of the simplest, cheapest, and most effective antidotes for stress that has ever been discovered is relaxation. The scientific evidence supporting the power of relaxation to counter the ravaging effects of stress diseases is overwhelming. So much so that it is difficult to know where to begin.

The scientific expert who has led the relaxation field is Dr. Edmund Jacobson. His book *You Must Relax* was originally published in 1934, and there have been many reprints.[2] Interestingly, Dr. Jacobson so accurately understood the value and technique of relaxation that his book has hardly needed to be updated since it was originally published.

Relaxation, intentionally and regularly practiced, is a powerful healing agent because it goes to the root of the problem. It helps our body shut down stress hormones and provides the right environment for healing the damage done by overstress. A close companion of relaxation needs to be meditation. It is also a powerful antidote for stress, which is why I am including it in this chapter. When relaxation (which is primarily the lowering of arousal in the body) is combined with meditation (which is primarily a lowering of arousal in the mind), you have a powerful cure for both stress and anxiety.

> One of the simplest, cheapest, and most effective antidotes for stress that has ever been discovered is relaxation.

RELAXATION TRAINING CD

In my *Relaxation Training* CD, I provide a series of relaxation and meditation exercises that are thoroughly scientific. These exercises are not only good for your body and mind but also for your spiritual life. They will help you to follow the injunction of God to the psalmist: "Be still, and know that I am God" (Ps. 46:10). Details on how to order this CD are provided at the end of this book.

Having made the case for the value of relaxation and meditation, let me now explore with you some insights and practical ways you can master these two important disciplines.

HOW RELAXATION WORKS

For many, the mere act of relaxing seems too simple a solution to restoring one's pleasure center to full functioning again. But it can. I am not exaggerating when I say that relaxation has the power to work miracles in our minds and bodies—for the simple reason that it significantly lowers the level of the stress hormones adrenaline and cortisol and, thus, helps to protects us from the damaging consequences of stress. So let me begin with a brief explanation of how relaxation works if only to convince you of its importance as a stress reliever.

Researchers, including myself, have demonstrated that relaxation lowers the body's level of arousal. The phenomenon has become known as the *relaxation response*, and it triggers the following consequences in our bodies:

* Reduction of the stress hormones, including adrenaline and cortisol

* Enhanced production of the brain's painkillers (called *endorphins*)

* Increased production of the brain's happy neurotransmitters

* Increased production of the brain's natural tranquilizers

* Increased immune system activity to fight off disease

* Reduction in blood pressure and a slowing down, if not elimination, of the hardening of the arteries

* Reduction in cholesterol levels, thus reducing the risk for heart disease

* Warming of the skin surface, especially of the hands and feet, due to relaxation of blood capillaries

If these benefits don't impress you, I don't know what will. And this is by no means a complete list of the identified benefits of relaxation and meditation.

That's the good news, now for the not-so-good news. Just sitting in your comfortable chair and reading the newspaper while watching your favorite TV program does not produce the relaxation response. Neither does playing golf, riding your motorcycle, or jogging. These recreational activities are good for something, but not relaxation.

In fact, many so-called recreational activities may even be creating increased stress through the increase adrenal arousal they produce. They are good for distraction from the troubles of your business or other challenges in life, but don't confuse their distraction value with the deeper need for real relaxation of the sort I am describing here.

MUSCLE RELAXATION EXERCISES

Most relaxation exercises focus on reducing muscle tension. They achieve this by forcing the muscles to be inactive for a period of time. However, relaxing muscles that have long been under tension is not as easy as it seems. In fact, many people find it almost impossible to relax their muscles without some help.

Biofeedback, short for *biological feedback*, uses scientific instruments that can measure various types of tension, such as muscle tension, elevated blood pressure, or cold hands. As a pioneer in the field of biofeedback, I have used these techniques for years to help my patients. When fed back this information, patients learn the correct relaxation for lowering those measures. Biofeedback is by far the best way to learn relaxation, but it is not always easily available—hence the *Relaxation Training* CD offered in the appendix.

The reason many people struggle to relax is that gradual buildup of muscle tension over the years has taken away their ability to sense or recognize their tension. This process is called accommodation, and it is extremely important that anyone starting on a relaxation program keep it in mind.

As you practice relaxation, especially when you get down to a deeper level of relaxation, deeper than your body has known for a long time, your tension will adapt back to its lower level. Then the

> Relaxation has the power to work miracles in our minds and bodies.

moment you become tense, your body will tell you. Persistence in reducing tension does pay off eventually with a greater awareness of your tense feelings so you can then deal with them.

So we are now ready to tackle a simple relaxation exercise. Don't undervalue it—it is powerful in its simplicity. Mastering this exercise and practicing it every day for thirty minutes will become a great benefit. You can then go on to more advanced relaxation exercises described in my *Relaxation and Christian Meditation* CD.

A RELAXATION EXERCISE

Preparation

Find a private place where you can sit or lie in a comfortable position. This could be done just sitting in your desk chair, in the bath, or in bed before you go to sleep at night.

Reflection

The goal is to take some uninterrupted time to focus on intentionally relaxing your body through muscle tensing and relaxing and slow, controlled breathing. Be aware of tension in your body, and intentionally release it so you can relax. You can do this before meditating and along with guided imagery to relax your mind.

Exercise

1. Close your eyes, take a deep breath, and focus on how and what your body feels. Start at the top of your head and proceed down toward your feet. If you notice any discomfort, make some adjustment in your position or add whatever will make you more comfortable. Do this now so you don't have to interrupt your relaxation later.

2. Now start to focus on relaxing all your muscles. Starting from your head, first tense your scalp muscles, hold the tension for a count of five, then relax them and leave them relaxed. Then move to your facial muscles and do the same. Then neck muscles, and proceed all the way down to your feet muscles, repeating the tension/relaxing procedure. Now remain relaxed and try not to move any muscles. Give them time to wind down.

3. Now, while relaxing your muscles, pay attention to your breathing. You will notice that you are breathing with your chest. You are breathing by expanding your chest cage. What you have to do now is switch to diaphragmatic breathing—breathing that is more conducive to relaxation. Breathing with your diaphragm occurs when your stomach rises with each breath, not your chest. So while breathing through your nose, move your stomach up, count to five, then slowly let the air out of your mouth as your stomach goes down.

> Many people find it almost impossible to relax their muscles without some help.

4. Continue to remain still for the remainder of your relaxing time,

ensuring that you are doing the diaphragmatic breathing exercise every four or five minutes. You could also now relax your mind, by imagining you are alone on a beautiful warm beach, and the warm waves of water are gently washing over you. Imagine how the sun and water feel on your skin, the fresh ocean smells, and the beauty and calm of the surroundings.

5. Achieving deep relaxation takes practice and patience, but keep doing it, and you will eventually gain the benefits. At first you might even feel restless and want to fidget; this is normal. Eventually, a deep relaxation state will emerge. You will start feeling more calm and relaxed. So persist in your relaxation, doing it at least once a day.

MEDITATION

Relaxation focuses on lowering muscle tension and calming the stress response system. Meditation relaxes the tension in your mind and soul, benefiting both the body and mind. As I mentioned earlier, you can combine relaxation with meditation.

Some form of meditation is found in nearly all religions. But the practice of meditation is by no means confined to any one religion and may even be practiced without any religious connotation whatsoever. In this chapter, I will focus on Christian contemplative meditation because this is where my faith and experience with meditation lies.

HOW DOES MEDITATION WORK?

Let me assume that you have never meditated and know little about it. As I have previously emphasized, relaxation helps to lower your muscle tension. Meditation helps to quiet the mind and induces relaxation throughout the body and soul. The calming effect alone has tremendous benefit whether or not used to enhance spiritual transformation.

Meditation is gaining credibility as an effective intervention for stress and anxiety management. When we meditate, we help the brain to become more tranquil by shutting down the arousal system through the release of natural tranquilizers produced within the brain, resulting in a calmer state. And this boost to the tranquility system helps us to restore balance in our pleasure center. It's impossible to be tense and stressed as well as calm and tranquil at the same time. So learn to let the calm take over and experience restoration and transformation.

> Meditation helps to quiet the mind and induces relaxation throughout the body and soul.

CHRISTIAN MEDITATION

Christian meditation involves a time of quiet contemplation with focused awareness on the presence of God. The focus is usually on a selected scripture or phrase that you prayerfully ponder over and over in your mind. Contemplative meditation is thinking with concentration about some topic. If you know how to worry, you are off to a good start. Meditation is a healthy form of worrying. You can just shift the focus, be a little more intentional, and before you know it, you will be enjoying the life-transforming, proven benefits from contemplative meditation.

Contemplative Christian meditation is also thought of as quiet prayer—a prayer of the heart without petition, since the Bible tells us that God already knows our needs (Matt. 6:8). Quiet, heartfelt prayers throughout the day bring our soul into a quiet rest and the body into a state of reduced tension. When you take all your longings and concerns to God in prayer, as well as remembering to be thankful for your blessings, your emotions and mind will be calmer, and you will experience more peace and tranquility in your life.

Contemplative meditation has the additional benefit of enhancing your awareness of God's presence and spiritual transformation. As you intentionally quiet your heart, focusing your mind on God and His Word, you permit the Holy Spirit to activate the life-giving Word of God in you, transforming your life to be more like Jesus.

> Contemplative meditation has the additional benefit of enhancing your awareness of God's presence and spiritual transformation.

How does contemplative meditation help restore a healthy pleasure center? Pursuing pleasure in God is what we were created for, and it is key to our overall health and spiritual growth. When your heart is satisfied in God's love and grace, you won't be as anxious, distracted, and lured by the fleeting pleasures of the world and sin as a substitute. Ultimately, God is most glorified in you when you are most satisfied in Him.

MEDITATION IS ESSENTIAL
TO HEALTHY CHRISTIAN LIVING

Catholics and Anglicans have a long history of enjoying contemplative meditation, and much of their worship style fosters opportunity for expression. Evangelicals, on the other hand, with increasing intensity have favored a stimulation-driven worship style. When many evangelical Christians go to church, they want an elevating fix, not a meditational downer.

I need to point out that a stimulation-driven spirituality is not conducive to lowered stress and tension or deeper transformation. In fact, many seek a fix when they go to church precisely because they are so stressed out all week that they cannot stand any lowering of their arousal on the weekend. It just puts them into a postadrenaline bad humor. Unfortunately, many churches don't teach and allow for contemplative practices, so Christians aren't integrating them into their life. A highly stressed lifestyle finds low arousal discomforting, so our evangelical mantra has become "Bring on the excitement, and I'll go to church!"

As you read this, I understand if you find yourself uncomfortable and resistant. Meditation may sound boring or like too much work. If you feel this way, you need to recognize that this perception is part of the anhedonia problem. If you can't enjoy stillness, you can't enjoy meditation. But don't let these misdirections turn you off. Remember, there are definite spiritual and physical benefits of meditating. I invite you to join with the many who are taking the meditational plunge and discovering why there is a resurgence of appreciation for the benefits of Christian contemplative meditation.

Fortunately, the practice of contemplative meditation is not totally foreign to evangelicals. Charles Haddon Spurgeon, the great preacher of the mid-1800s who is affectionately called the Prince of Preachers, strongly advocated meditation. He particularly encouraged meditating on Scripture, and we could well benefit from his encouragement here. In a sermon on meditation, he said the person who merely listens to many sermons "is not necessarily well-instructed in the faith." You can read many books and still not be a "better scholar in Christ's school."[3]

DIFFERENT FORMS OF CHRISTIAN CONTEMPLATIVE MEDITATION AND PRAYER

From the earliest days of the church, Christians have used meditation as an essential part of Bible reading and prayer along with worship and praise. Meditation offers a time to intentionally focus on God in His works and words before we fall asleep, upon awaking, or throughout the day.

Here are a few examples of Christian contemplative meditation and prayer:

* *Lectio divina.* Meditating on the Scriptures. Coming to know who God really is and cultivating friendship with Christ.

* *Devotional reading.* Reflecting on liturgy, hymns, worship songs, inspirational writings.

* *Practicing the presence of God.* Developing a continual openness and awareness of Christ living in you and God's presence in your life.

* *Developing a contemplative lifestyle.* Prioritizing spiritual transformation, personal relationship with God, and the things that really matter.

* *Silence, solitude, and listening prayer.* Being free from noise, distractions, and people to totally enter into time alone with God, to open yourself up to Him.

* *Gratitude.* Remembering God's blessings in your life. Focusing feelings of gratitude in your physical heart. Expressing gratefulness to others.

* *The Jesus prayer.* Repeating the phrase "Lord Jesus Christ, Son of God, have mercy on me, a sinner" in heartfelt prayer.

* *Examen.* Daily reflecting on what you are most grateful for (consolation) and what you are least grateful for (desolation).

* *Breath prayer.* Presenting simple, heartfelt desires before God.

* *Centering prayer.* Connecting with God in a real way, consenting to God's presence and action within.

* *Contemplative prayer.* Opening your heart, mind, and whole being to the awareness of God, honestly and authentically. A process of interior purification and character transformation.

* *Prayer walking.* Aligning yourself and opening yourself to Christ while walking and praying for His kingdom to come.

I won't be able to cover all these forms of Christian meditation, so for further exploration, please refer to the appendix at the end of the book. In this chapter, I will focus on just two: meditating on Scripture and practicing the presence of God. These two classic spiritual exercises will help you begin to learn Christian contemplative meditation, enhancing body-mind calmness and enriching spiritual transformation. Using a journal to note reflections and experiences will add to the benefits of your meditations.

MEDITATING ON SCRIPTURE

One form of Christian meditation that has been widely used since at least the fourth century AD is the *lectio divina*, which centers on loving God and being transformed through His Word. Traditionally used in monastic religious orders, it is having resurgence today, and many evangelicals are being drawn to it.

Over the centuries this practice has become widely appreciated as a way of enriching and transforming one's faith life. Even evangelicals now find it valuable to balance well-established practices that emphasize Bible study and nonliturgical worship services. If you are an evangelical, like myself, you might find this practice most helpful and uplifting. After all, it's God you are focusing on.

Lectio divina simply means *sacred reading*. It has four stages: *lectio* (reading), *meditatio* (meditation), *oratio* (affective prayer), and *contemplatio* (contemplation).

First, a particular passage is read (*lectio*). Then time is spent pondering the text (*meditatio*). This leads to prayer (*oratio*), talking to God about the reading, asking Him to reveal truth to you. The final stage (*contemplatio*) is simply a resting in God's presence.

Preparation

Select a comfortable place and position, either inside or outside, that will be your sanctuary for the meditation. Set aside some uninterrupted time, starting with about twenty minutes. There is no time limit, so you may choose a shorter time to begin with and take more extended time when you can. Just meditate on a scriptural passage until you feel you have completed it. Many find that first thing in the morning and in the evening provide the most practical opportunities for this.

Reflection

Meditating on Scripture is not the same as studying Scripture. The goal is not head knowledge but heart knowledge. You are opening to a deeper understanding of the meaning to you personally, listening and welcoming God's presence into your life. You are entering into the spirit of the text to receive and respond.

Exercise

1. *Read the passage of Scripture (lectio).* Begin the exercise by selecting a portion of Scripture. The passage could be from a teaching you recently heard, a daily devotional reading, a passage coinciding with reading through the Bible in a year, or a favorite portion. To illustrate, I will use a scripture reading that lends itself to meditation: Psalm 23. While you probably know this psalm by heart, start by reading Psalm 23. Read it slowly and deliberately. The first few verses are:

> The LORD is my shepherd, I shall not be in want.
> He makes me lie down in green pastures,
> he leads me beside quiet waters,
> he restores my soul. (vv. 1–3)

2. *Meditate on the passage (meditatio).* Now break the portion down into short, meaningful phrases. For instance, I would break it down as follows:

* The Lord
* Is my shepherd
* I shall not be in want
* He makes me lie down
* In green pastures
* He leads me
* Beside quiet waters
* He restores my soul

Focus on each phrase. Then repeat the phrase to yourself, silently or out loud, several times. Allow it to sink in and prompt your thoughts about it.

Now reflect on a phrase: for example, "The Lord." Personalize it. He is *my* Lord. What thoughts does personalizing it conjure up for you? Lordship over *my* life. Ask yourself questions such as *How is my life touched by this passage? What does this suggest to me? What does* lord of my life *practically look like in my life? How do I feel about that?* Try keeping your mind still and focused. Just contemplate His lordship over your life, your family, and the universe.

Ask the Holy Spirit to speak within you; invite Christ to be formed in you while deliberating on the words. Free associate and let your thoughts go where they lead you regarding the passage. Go through each phrase reflecting similarly as time permits.

3. *Pray the scriptural passage (oratio).* Out of your reading, reflection, and meditation, how does it call you to respond to God speaking to you? This is a subtle transition and may be woven in unnoticed. It is basically your heart response to the Scripture you have been focusing your mind on. Your understanding of the passage moves deeper into personalizing and internalizing it through prayers like "Show me how . . .," "Thank You for . . .," and "Help me . . ." This moves you into an obedient, embracing response.

4. *Contemplate the scriptural passage (contemplatio).* During the final phase, simply rest in God. This is active *waiting on the Lord* in full attention, alertness, and hope. Don't be concerned about results or feelings. Just be present with God. When your mind wanders, center yourself quietly by repeating a key word or phrase from the text or picturing an image of the text to return to the spirit of the passage. Before finishing, you may want to journal the insights that have come to you to pursue in your next meditation session.

Take as long as you need, weaving in prayer and contemplation, until you feel you have completed your meditation time or until you need to stop due to other time commitments. You can always pick up where you left off next time.

Helpful Suggestions

1. If you are a type A extrovert personality or if you are experiencing severe anhedonia, this time of quiet and silence may be difficult for you at first. You may feel restless and have a hard time focusing your mind. That is normal. Just accept it and try to focus on not rushing, analyzing, or intellectualizing. Intentionally set your mind on the things that are true and lovely and that open you up to God.

2. Start with shorter times of meditation that are more doable so that you don't get too frustrated and give up. Just keep giving it a try. As you practice, you will slowly get the gist of it and reap the healing, life-changing benefits.

3. Remember that meditation is a process—a journey, not a destination. It is not a structured Bible study, so just relax, be patient, don't judge yourself, and let God guide your thoughts.

PRACTICING THE PRESENCE OF GOD

Another form of Christian meditation is practicing the presence of God. This awakens our awareness of God's presence in all things, restfully opening up to Him, enabling us to always be with God—just as we are.

Practicing the presence of God is often associated with the seventeenth-century French monk Brother Lawrence. He longed to maintain an ongoing conversation and to find pleasure in God no matter what He was doing. He discovered inward and outward pleasure and joy by making it his business to rest in Christ's holy presence through habitual conversation with God. He learned a way of living with a deeper awareness of God's presence in his life as you can as well.

Unfortunately, anhedonia resulting from damage to the pleasure center dampens our created desire and pleasure to love and worship God, to enjoy the freedom and fullness of life He desires for us. The soul and spirit are left wondering if you will ever sense God's presence, if you'll ever get anything meaningful and helpful out of faith, and if spiritual dryness is going to be permanent.

In the midst of our busy, scattered, exhausted, and hurting lives, we can become desperate to experience a great love with God. Fortunately, we can rekindle the healthy pleasure we were created for. Practicing the presence of God is a way to recover your life in the uncertainty and bombardment of modern living, being aware and connected to God in a real way.

A life devoted to God should also be a life devoted to the pleasure of reveling in Him and remembering who He is, all He has done and is doing around you. While

> We need to keep our eyes and ears open to God—go on a God hunt throughout the day.

Christian believers trust that God is always with them, we seldom intentionally try to increase our awareness of His presence and find pleasure in Him by turning our minds to Him and setting aside some unhurried time to connect with Him. We need to keep our eyes and ears open to God—go on a *God hunt* throughout the day. Following are some beginning suggestions on how you can pursue the pleasure of God's presence in your life.

Reflection

Developing an intentional, continual awareness of God's presence in you and around you will bring more calm to your heart and help restore finding pleasure in Him. Learning to stay in the presence of God can be experienced in many ways, such as through breath prayer, the Lord's Prayer, or centering prayer. The focus is not on a strategy or ritual but on personal relationship. It is simply a way to love God, find pleasure in Him, and stay connected throughout all the good and challenging events of your day.

Preparation

These few questions can help prepare your heart to being more aware of God's presence. If you feel distant and disconnected from God, do you long to experience His love and joy and find more pleasure in Him? What would it look like in your life to intentionally be open to a deeper intimacy with God? Have you ever had an awareness of God in your life and enjoyed His presence? How easy would it be for God to get your attention?

When is it best for you to hear God's still, small voice? We all have times of wandering, drifting, and getting clogged up with the worries of the world. Consider some of the ways to experience a clearer pathway to pleasure in God's presence.

Exercise

1. Begin by gently turning your heart toward God, expressing your intention to live in union with Him. Whatever task you are doing, dedicate it to God, talking to Him before you begin, during, and after.
2. At the beginning of the day, offer yourself and the day to God with the intention of being more aware of His presence. You might reflect

on the Lord's Prayer, meditating on a phrase such as "Your kingdom come, Your will be done in my life." Say in your heart, "Lord, I am here. Help me listen and be aware of Your presence." At the end of the day, reflect on how you were more aware of God's presence in and around you.

3. Before going to bed, reflect on three things that went well in the day, why you think they went well, and how you were aware of God's presence. With a heart of gratitude, write down these three blessings every night for a week, meditating on them as you go to sleep. You will sleep better and have more pleasant dreams. In the morning, anticipate three things that will go well, and how you will look for God's presence throughout the day.

4. As you go through the day, be aware of songs, ideas, Scriptures, people, and gestures of kindness that cross your mind. Could these be God's Spirit prompting you, being near to you?

5. Develop a collection of your own prayers, Scriptures, sayings, and songs that you can reflect on while driving, showering, walking, or working. Allow these to draw you deeper into awareness and encounters with God.

6. As you are going about your work in the day, experiencing a concern or interruption, simply hold out your hands, turn it over to God, and invite Him into the situation. The following prayers will help you stay present with God.

The Breath Prayer

The Breath Prayer is also known as *prayer of the heart*. Sit or lie comfortably, intentionally pondering the nearness of God and the rhythm of your breathing. As you deeply breathe in, think or say a name of God, and as you breathe out, voice thankfulness, a deep desire or concern on your heart. Breathe in *Shepherd*, and breathe out *lead me by still waters*. Breathe in *Father*, breathe out *Your will be done in me*. Breathe in *Healer*, breathe out *restore my soul*.

Another option is to repeat a one-sentence prayer followed by a word or phrase expressing what is on your heart. Connect the prayer with your breathing, and return to this throughout your day. Phrases often used are "My soul glorifies the Lord" (Luke 1:46); "My soul finds rest in God alone" (Ps. 62:1); "Shepherd, lead me by still waters" (see Ps. 23:2 KJV); or "Come, Holy Spirit."

The Jesus Prayer

Begin by sitting comfortably in solitude and silence. Close your eyes and breathe softly, calming your thoughts and body. Let your thoughts flow from your mind to your heart, softly saying, "Lord Jesus Christ, have mercy on me." You can say this in your mind or whisper it gently over and over again. Another variation is to breathe in praying "Jesus, Son of David," and breathe out saying, "Have mercy on me, a sinner." This is meant to be a breathing rhythm of surrender, reminding you of God's presence.

Helpful Suggestions

1. Begin and end each day with a breath prayer.
2. If there is someone you are praying for, as a phrase or prayer comes to your mind during the day, offer it up to the Lord. You don't have to say long, complicated prayers. God will hear your prayer of the heart.
3. Remember that you are more likely to hear what God has to say through His still, small voice than through a big megaphone experience. You will be more aware of God's presence by noticing and being grateful for the ordinary, simple happenings in your day.

A HEALTHY APPROACH
TO CHRISTIAN MEDITATION

In closing this chapter, let me say a word of encouragement to those Christians who are uncomfortable with the idea of meditation. I have been active in conservative Christian circles for most of my life and have frequently encountered strong resistance to the idea of meditation. Some believe it is New Age stuff, others that any kind of meditation is dangerous and mind-altering. One pastor once said to me, "There is a difference between reading the Word and understanding its meaning versus focusing on a single word to gain a mystical experience." Obviously, he could not appreciate how going beyond reading the Word and meditating on it can be spiritually beneficial.

It is true that some use meditation merely to achieve a mystical experience. However, this is not the approach I have presented here. I believe that there is a healthy approach to meditation that can be both spiritually and emotionally helpful to even the most ardent conservative believer. I encourage you to be open to a genuine experience of Christian meditation. It will enhance your experience of God significantly—and keep your pleasure system in good shape.

STEP 7—MAKE SPACE FOR THE THINGS THAT MATTER

Before you know it, a sense of God's wholeness,
everything coming together for good,
will come and settle you down.
—THE APOSTLE PAUL (PHIL. 4:7 MSG)

Our lives are too cluttered. We have gadgets, clothes, books, mementos, and possessions of all kinds. We are also chaotically cluttered with bad habits and pursuits that really don't amount to anything important in the larger scheme of things. The so-called hallmarks of the modern busy life are not all they are cracked up to be. If anything, they conspire to fill up every inch of our space and the moments of every day with meaningless distractions that divert us from the things that really matter. And I am as guilty as anyone.

Sometimes it takes a life tragedy to push us back on to the right tracks of our lives. To me, it happened thirteen years ago when my son-in-law,

Richard, father of two of my grandsons, had his young life tragically cut short. A schoolteacher, he was driving to work when a crate fell off a truck in front of him. He swerved to miss the crate but lost control of the car and it plunged over the edge of the freeway, ending his life.

> Sometimes it takes a life tragedy to push you back on to the right tracks of your life.

What a painful time it was for all of us. I grieved for Richard. I grieved for my daughter, widowed at age thirty-four. I grieved for my two young grandsons, who had been robbed of years of fun with a dad they loved. And I grieved for my wife, who had developed a deep spiritual relationship with Richard.

But at that same time, something profound happened deep inside me. I was preoccupied with things like my career and wanting to be more successful as a writer. I was focused on what I didn't have and wanted and what I did have but regretted. All told, I was certainly not a contented person. Sure, I was a Christian and believed in all the right things, but life itself had become a little too complicated for my own good. Pleasure? You must be joking. My life was too cluttered with meaningless distractions for anything to give me any deep sense of real and abiding gratification.

Standing at Richard's graveside, two realizations overwhelmed me. First, life is short and unpredictable. I had always known that. My grandmother had drummed it into me. But somehow it had never penetrated deep into my very bones as it did standing at my son-in-law's graveside. Second, when death strikes unexpectedly, all the clutter and accumulations of your life don't amount to a hill of beans. Not money, not possessions, not even one's lofty dreams of success. Death screams loud and clear, "Get your priorities right, my friend, if you want to live a contented life!"

From that moment on, I have had a profound feeling that there is very little on this earth that really matters besides the relationships we have with one another. And what do we have to do in order to extract meaningful pleasure from our existence? I am convinced it is quite simple: make space for the things that really matter. That's what this chapter is all about.

PLEASURE'S DETRACTORS

Outside of a handful of scientists, modern anhedonia is relatively unrecognized and certainly not commonly acknowledged. It has not come upon us with great fanfare, but is a reality of modern life nevertheless.

Don't you find it heartbreaking that so many people, including our own children and future grandchildren, will go through a whole life never having experienced the deep delight of being alive? Most of them are already bogged down in a quagmire of disappointment, addiction, sickness, or pain. And any whisper of enduring happiness is too soft to be heard. Many (at least one in three) will inevitably suffer from preventable physical distress later in their lives. Others (one in five) will experience a devastating depression. And as we now know, personal physical distress can as easily cause emotional trauma. And the consequences of emotional trauma can flood far and wide, drowning families and friends in a sea of misery. I don't know of any family that has suffered from a major traumatic event that is now full of joyfulness. Even though we were designed to be resilient, few regain all their pretrauma capacity for pleasurable living. Sad, but an eye-opener for all of us.

> Make space for the things that really matter.

DO WE CAUSE OUR OWN MISERY?

Life can be cruel and deliver some devastating blows. But is our misery entirely the fault of some terrible trauma—something that has happened to us? I don't think so. Most of us are victims of our own ill-designed coping abilities. We bring misery on ourselves. As someone has said, "Many people die because they did not learn how to live." In other words, they die physically and emotionally because they lacked the understanding and determination to choose to live healthy, happy, prosperous lives, despite horrendous circumstances in their pasts.

So, yes, we do cause a lot of our own misery. This is why the phenomenon of victimization is so prevalent in our Western culture. Everyone sees themselves as victims of circumstances beyond their control. We tend to see ourselves as helpless pawns in the game of life, the victims of what others do, and then we settle down into a self-soothing misery. We blame our parents or someone else for destroying our ambitions. This seemingly endless cycle of resentment and despair will not go away without some attention.

Something has to change, and since we cannot change our past or the potential for life to stop delivering traumatic blows, we are left with only one option: change ourselves. We must learn to *get over it*, whatever *it* is, and then learn to live with it, making a new start with new choices. We need to rise up from the ashes of our despair and embrace a new life. No matter how bad your circumstances, you cannot blame them for your general unhappiness. You have to look within yourself and find where your ability to experience pleasure is being blocked.

I know this is a tall order, but for people of faith, in particular, it should be cause for hope. Scripture again and again shouts out one very important principle (forgive the cliché, but it is true): when the going gets tough, the tough get going! For example, James 1:2–4 says, "Is your life full of difficulties and temptations? Then be happy, for when the way is rough, your patience has a chance to grow. So let it grow, and don't try to squirm out of your problems. For when your patience is finally in full bloom, then you will be ready for anything, strong in character, full and complete" (TLB).

> We need to rise up from the ashes of our despair and embrace a new life.

What does this have to do with the healing of our pleasure system? A lot! A victimization mentality, coupled with our inability to get over the bad circumstances in our life, destroys our capacity for experiencing any real enjoyment or gratification. Pleasure can only be found in a contented, peaceful, unresentful, nondespairing person who has put the past behind him or her, has embraced the future with hope, and is living life free of its past burdens. How you cope with life can make or break your pleasure system.

Life should be a magnificent experience for all of us. That's what it was designed to be. But achieving the full magnificence of life will take a fight. Authentic happiness does not come easily. The battle lines are drawn between pushing forward or surrendering in despair, and our future happiness, as well as the happiness of those we touch daily, is at stake. How well you recover from a life of tragedy ultimately depends upon your willingness to take responsibility for this recovery, not for your circumstances but for your reaction to them. It's all about putting it behind you.

MOVE OVER, ALL BAD THINGS

There are many circumstances we may just have to learn to live with. Putting them behind us may not be possible. But even in the midst of bad circumstances, we have to find space in our lives for those things that really matter. In other words, we have to push aside the bad things so that we can make room for the good things. It's all a matter of getting your priorities right.

By and large, life becomes more painful when we have unbalanced priorities—when we pursue unhealthy goals and neglect the essential building blocks for a life of contentment and joyfulness. Or to put it in scientific terms, unless you send the right life ingredients to your pleasure center, don't expect it to deliver the happiness goods.

So as I close this book, I want to highlight what I consider to be the right ingredients for a life that can experience the full flow of healthy pleasure. These are the ones that I have found to be the most challenging, not just for myself but also for the many clients I have worked with over the years. Whatever else you do, make room for what is to follow.

MAKE ROOM FOR GOD
AND SPIRITUAL PRIORITIES

This is where I have to begin, because it is so important. And please understand where I am coming from. I am *not* here to proselytize; I abhor that as much as anyone. But the fact is that without a spiritual base for your life, you have no foundation on which to build, just an empty hole.

> We do the best we can with the brokenness we bring to God.

For many thinking people, issues of faith and God are problematic because they don't believe a person can really know whether God exists. Profound doubts get in the way of many so that they don't even begin to explore the value of, say, Christianity and faith. Also, I can't say that those who give witness to our Christian faith always epitomize the best of our faith. Sorry about this, but God didn't come to save the perfect, only the rest of us who are imperfect. So stop expecting Christians to practice what they preach all the time. We do the best we can with the brokenness we bring to God. The best of us Christians struggle in our faith and doubts just like others.

I had a dear friend and colleague, a very prestigious professor of ethics, who was about the most honest Christian I know. I doubt if there is any-one more open about how difficult it is to build a faith-based Christian life than he was. He passed away at the same time that I was having bypass surgery three years ago. He fell off a ladder, hit his head on the driveway, and died a few days later. His name was Lewis Smedes—a well-known author with several outstanding books, including *Forgive and Forget*, which reached the *New York Times* bestsellers list.

> You have to hope in something, because any hope is better than no hope at all.

Despite his brilliant intellect, or perhaps because of it, he would often express how powerfully he had experienced doubt about his faith earlier in his life. He had to cling tenaciously to his faith as a Christian most of his life. This is how he expressed his struggle in a short autobiography that he had completed just weeks before he died: "Sometimes I hang on to faith by my fingernails; when the dream of a new world of Jesus' peace and love is more than two thousand years old and still shows no sign of coming true, anybody's faith is bound to doubt."

Yet despite these doubts (and I am sure we all have them at times), he confesses that he could never give up his faith. "Without Jesus we are stuck with two options: utopian illusion or deadly despair. I scorn illusion. I dread despair. So I put all my money on Jesus!"

If those of us who are people of faith are wrong and we are nothing but a bunch of gullible dunces, we still win more than we lose. The odds are clearly in our favor. You have to hope in something because any hope is better than no hope at all. You have to have faith in something because without faith in anything, there is no point in living. You are dead inside from the start. "So," says Lewis Smedes, "I put all my eggs in one basket." [1] Gladly I do the same and make plenty of space for God. It's the best show in town.

MAKE ROOM FOR FRIENDSHIPS

When I was a teenager in South Africa, I had three very special friends. We called ourselves the Four Musketeers. We went everywhere and did everything together. We were inseparable—blood brothers. We had all become Christians in our early teens, and that helped to bond us in a very significant way. In fact, we formed a quartet and would sing at youth meetings.

Then we grew up and each of us pursued different careers. One became a dentist, two became mining engineers, and I became a civil engineer and then switched to studying clinical psychology in my late twenties. We all married and went our separate ways to different parts of the world.

While I have formed many other friendships over the years since then, I have never established the same level of friendship as we had as the Four Musketeers. Partly this is because the teenage years provide the most opportunity for bonding in friendship. Our brains are wired for this during this period. But more importantly, something has changed in our modern culture that is making it increasingly difficult to form close adult friendships, outside of one's spouse (and some even struggle here). Sure, you make friends, but they are not the same depth of friendship you develop in early life.

So it is no surprise that a study conducted by sociologists at Duke University and the University of Arizona shows that Americans are slowly giving up on friendship. People just do not have as many friends as they used to. And this is not just true for adults; it is true for teenagers as well. Good-bye to the Four Musketeers!

What is the reason for this decline in close friendships? The same reason as that which produces our profound anhedonia: we do not find people as pleasurable in our hurried, stress-driven lives as people did in times past. For me, my childhood friendships meant everything. We would have died for one another—or that is how we felt.

The Duke study began as an attempt to debunk a previous study outlined in a provocative book published by a Harvard professor, called *Bowling Alone*. He portrayed society as becoming an increasingly lonely society. The Duke sociologists questioned his thesis and set out to debunk it. To their surprise, however, the researchers discovered that their study actually gave vindication to the provocative book. We are becoming more isolated. By choice or otherwise, we are increasingly becoming loners even in our closest and most intimate relationships. It is now known as the *modern alienation* problem—and is showing a dramatic increase.

What is causing this trend? For one thing, people are spending more time networking on the Internet than they are in face-to-face relationships. On the Web, you can share photographs, send e-mails, join chat groups, and create your own blog (short for *Web log*) to build a stable of friends without even leaving your bedroom. But is this really what friendships are all about? Can you cry on a blogger's shoulder? Can you find comfort in the arms of an e-mail? I can assure you that e-mail and text-messaging do not have the same cathartic effect as a *heart-to-heart*—as the Brits call it.

Let's be clear about what real friendship is all about. There aren't enough words to describe the profoundness of a friend. I have friends who are my neighbors, friends in other countries, friends I know from school, friends I worked with, favorite friends, friends I adore. To some extent, all of these people have been friends, but only a few are or were real friends.

> Renew your efforts in building long-term friendships, and then hold on to them for all you are worth.

Real friends are the people you can call on when you are in trouble—and I don't mean just family members. They are the people you want to spend time with, go places with, even die with. They know all of your horrible secrets yet still stick with you no matter what. They support you through every trial. And most important of all, they don't expect anything in return other than your friendship. Don't you long for such friendships?

Obviously, a true friendship doesn't develop overnight. And this is why one has to be intentional and make room for such relationships. If you are not intentional about it, it will never happen. So renew your efforts in building long-term friendships, and then hold on to them for all you are worth.

MAKE ROOM FOR FAMILY

While friendships are important, your extended family is even more important. Single or married, widowed or divorced, the research is clear: there has to be a family connection in your life if you are going to thrive. Believe me, your brain and sanity demand it.

If you are married, having a good relationship with your spouse is of vital importance, so work hard at building the best one you can. If you need help, see the book I wrote with my daughter, *Safe Haven Marriage*.[2] Remember, divorce doesn't fix everything. (I know; my parents divorced when I was twelve years old, and life only got worse.) Divorce is as likely to occur in remarriage as in the first marriage, for one reason: if you don't change, you carry all your dysfunctional baggage into the new marriage. Far better to try to make the first marriage work.

But while the quality of the marriage relationship is important, a more serious problem is the one I want to focus on here: the fast track most parents and kids are on is not conducive to finding room for family. You may get to the destination station faster, but you will have missed the passing scenery on the way.

A recent *Time* magazine article entitled "Ready, Set, Relax!" says it all.[3] The author tells the story of a mom who, just a few weeks before, after picking up her daughter from school, committed an act of soccer-mom heresy. Instead of heading to soccer practice, she drove her daughter to the local bookstore, where they whiled away two and a half hours listening to Lemony Snicket—the daughter's favorite author—read from his new book. Then, instead of snatching a fast-food dinner from a drive-through window so they could rush off to their next activity, they drove home and, joined by her older brother, leisurely cooked burgers on the family grill. "She's only ten, and there are plenty more years left for soccer," explained the mother, "but not another opportunity to meet Lemony Snicket." That's making room for family. It's all about having your priorities right.

Moms and dads everywhere are worn out from dragging their kids through the frenzied after-school ritual of dinners-on-the-go and crosstown-SUV-shuttle-runs between practices, competitions, private lessons, and club meetings. But the *Time* magazine report tells of a group of folks who decided to change this. Two years ago, they launched "Ready, Set, Relax!" and it became a citywide initiative that encouraged frazzled families to put down some speed bumps in their fast-paced lives. Now, this is a revolution I would support.

Years of multitasking and workaholism have left Americans across the economic and geographic spectrum feeling exhausted. (And, I might add, anhedonic as well.) This is the problem: not enough time for family. And the consequences for the happiness of our children are as obvious as the noses on our faces.

What can you, as a parent, do about this? Here are a few practical suggestions:

* Schedule regular times when you can just sit down with your kids and listen to their stories—about their day, school, friends, ambitions, etc. If you don't schedule it, it won't happen.

* Talk openly with your kids about their overextension and what you can do about it.

* Put your foot down firmly whenever you sense that your kids are being overwhelmed. Our children can sometimes be their own worst enemies.

* Plan for regular family outings—no other friends, just your family. You will encounter resistance from your kids—that's for sure—because they always want to be with their friends first. But insist that this time is just for your family and that they can hang out with their friends at another time.

* Try your utmost to always eat dinner together. Family members who eat dinner together have a much better chance of achieving a joyful life.

✻ Place a limit on the number of times you come home late from work. Sure, there may be times you can't help it, but unless you are determined to give first priority to your family, you will always fail here.

MAKE ROOM FOR FORGIVENESS

Forgiveness may seem out of place in the topic of pleasure, but trust me: it is as important to your pleasure center as anything else I know. If science is teaching us anything, it is helping us understand that the age-old importance that the Bible places on the act of forgiveness is really justified. The apostle Paul's words of advice are as powerful and relevant today as they have ever been: "Get rid of all bitterness, rage and anger, brawling and slander, along with any form of malice. Be kind and compassionate to one another, forgiving each other, just as in Christ God forgave you" (Eph. 4:31–32).

I would even go so far as to say that this advice is even more relevant today than at any time in history. Why do I say this? Because recent research utilizing modern brain-scanning techniques reveal that the ability to forgive and give up grudges is a key buffer against emotional and mental disease.[4] Do you want to live longer, happier, more contented, and with a fully functioning pleasure center? Then follow the apostle Paul's advice here. The fantastic ability we now have to scan the human brain and observe its functioning in more detail is opening up a whole new way of learning important lessons about the power of forgiveness.

What does forgiveness do for us? For starters, it relieves our anger, which is a primary factor in the development of early heart disease. Relieving anger also reduces our stress hormones, notably the adrenaline that bats around our body as we look for a fight or a way to take revenge for the hurt done to us. And when forgiving reduces our stress hormones, including cortisol, the hormone that can damage our emotional systems, it also protects our pleasure system from becoming anhedonic through the overstimulation of the pleasure pathways.

The bottom line is this: unresolved and unforgiving anger that can grow into persistent grudge-bearing destroys our capacity for joy and happiness. Anger might make you feel better in one part of your life, but in all else you will be miserable.

For many of us, anger is an emotion we experience far too often. The stress of modern life is characterized by high levels of frustration, and even kindergarten children know that this leads to anger. Take a toy car from me that I prefer playing with as opposed to listening to the teacher, and I will throw a temper tantrum the likes of which could go down in the history books. Then, by the time I am grown up, I will have learned how to turn small infractions into giant betrayals, and betrayals into grudges that not even an industrial-grade detergent could wipe away.

> The ability to forgive and give up grudges is a key buffer against emotional and mental disease.

Worse still, anger and resentment keep us captive to ruminations and fantasies of revenge. With all this anger batting around, small pleasures don't have a chance. They will drown in a sea of bitter feelings that cannot coexist with simple pleasures. When anger enters, welcome anhedonia; good-bye happiness.

But what is forgiveness? Basically, when somebody does something wrong—either against an individual or against the society—forgiveness means pardoning the accused with no resentment left. If forgiveness is complete, the offense is totally forgotten, as if it never took place.

Since many struggle to know precisely what they have to do in order to forgive, let me give you my definition of forgiveness. It is described in several of my books, written well before the present-day emphasis on the power of forgiveness. But it is worth mentioning again.

I learned it from a preacher in South Africa when I was in my early twenties and thought I knew everything there was to know about life. We were chatting about the terrible things going on in South Africa. I had expressed the view that there was no way we could ever undo the damage that apartheid had done. He replied that there was a way— the way of forgiveness—that could work that miracle.

> If forgiveness is complete, the offense is totally forgotten, as if it never took place.

Fifty years later, forgiveness did work that miracle through the Truth and Reconciliation Commission set up by Bishop Tutu and others. And it was that preacher, who befriended me many years ago, who offered the following definition of *forgiveness*: forgiveness is surrendering my right to hurt you back. In essence, forgiveness is not a feeling (you may feel no better afterward). Rather, it is an act of the will in which you let go of your natural desire to take revenge for the hurt that has been done to you.

LET GO OF GRUDGES

An aspect of forgiveness that is often overlooked is that once you have genuinely forgiven, you have to let go of any grudges you might continue to feel. It may not happen immediately, but in the course of time it can. Letting go of grudges has become a very important topic in positive psychology, a movement that is now revolutionizing psychology. If you want to know more about it, just look up *positive psychology* or *Dr. Martin Seligman*—the founder of this movement—on the Internet.

Dr. Seligman started to explore letting go of grudges by experimenting with *forgiveness letters*. In these letters, a person who feels wronged is encouraged to write a letter of forgiveness to the offending party. Not an idea I would suggest—as I had stated many years ago when writing on this topic—and it failed horribly in these experiments. The problem is that the person receiving the letter always felt offended. They had not asked for forgiveness, so why was it being offered? In many cases, the apparent offender didn't even believe that he or she had done any offending or that the accusation was justified. So the forgiveness letters only contributed more hurt to the original hurt.

> Forgiveness is surrendering my right to hurt you back.

In its place, therefore, researchers began to focus on the person feeling offended. I've always believed this. Forgiveness is not for the benefit of the one who has done the hurting, but for the one who has been hurt. When we forgive, we forgive so that we might be healed of our grudge. Sounds selfish, but that's how it works. And that is how the New Testament in the Bible presents it.

So psychologists studying this area came up with the *letting go of grudges* exercise. It is really an exercise in forgiveness, but it focuses on the offended, not the offender. When you let go of your grudge, you remove the unhappy, bitter feelings that block your ability to take pleasure in your life.

The goal of this exercise is not to excuse the behavior of the one who has hurt you but to help you forgive and forget it. Slowly, you reduce the need to ruminate, and over time the hurt assumes less importance. The goal is to help you shift your focus from grudging to gratitude. You can turn off the grudge feeling by turning on your feelings of gratitude. The two cannot coexist. The one displaces the other. By widening your focus to include the larger picture of the other party, you can restore a healthy perspective on the hurt. Gratitude also undoes the effects of your anger.

Dr. Karen Reivich developed the following exercise to help adolescents and adults overcome grudges:

Step 1. Start by choosing someone in your life you know well and against whom you have a grudge. Doesn't have to be a big one—you can experiment with something small just to master the practice. On a sheet of paper, draw a circle in the center and inside that circle state the essence of your grudge in just a few words. For example, let's say it is your spouse (just to bring the exercise close to home), and you feel that he or she is not being responsive to your need for intimacy. Or it can be your best friend who has let you down.

> Once you have genuinely forgiven, you have to let go of any grudges you might continue to feel.

Step 2. Now fill the rest of the page with blank circles. Draw at least ten of them, but not more than fifteen. Now fill each of these circles with a word or phrase that describes something about the person who has hurt you for which you are grateful. It can be something he or she said to you, an unselfish act of kindness, a compliment, something important about the relationship, small things, big things, current things, past things. Take a little time to choose them carefully. Your anger might try to block out anything good, but shut it down for now.

Step 3. After you have filled in all the circles, hold the sheet at arm's length. Notice how the grudge circle gets lost in the sea of gratitude.

Step 4. Now reflect on whether your feelings toward the other person have changed—even just a little. You see, all you have to do is change your focus, and the crack in the grudge door opens a little. The inflow of gratitude begins to dilute your anger. Notice whether the grudge has weakened? Do you find your perspective on it changing? Can you now find a way to talk about your hurt without reoffending? What positive aspects of the relationship can you start to build on? Can you just let it all go in an act of forgiveness?

Now (and this is very important), either destroy the sheet or file it in a confidential place where it cannot be found. You don't want the other person to find it, lest it only cause them offense.

MAKE ROOM FOR FAILURE AND DISAPPOINTMENT

Of all the things we need to make room for, making room for failure is perhaps the most vexing. Next to death, the other great certainty of life is that sooner or later we will all experience failure and disappointment—and not too many people I know have made room for this in their lives. And if there is one life event that can play havoc with our happiness and pleasure, it is the sense of having failed or being extremely disappointed. Maybe I am just speaking for myself here, but there is no joy in one's soul when life lets you down.

No one can go through a whole life without some letdown or disappointment, let alone a major failure. I have known clients who, after several years of great success in which they had made enough money to retire, have lost it all. Everything. But they were resilient and bounced back because they understood one very important life principle: failures are to grow by. If you make room for failure, you can overcome it. The effect of such failure is usually one of devastation because the victim has not embraced failure as an element of good living.

I have discussed the topic of failure in several of my books, notably in *Fifteen Principles for Achieving Happiness*[5] and in *Habits of the Mind*,[6] so I do not want to repeat what I have written there. Let me summarize some key principles for how you can make room for the failure in your life—room that I trust will give you good bounce-back-ability. Resiliency is the name of the game when it comes to failure.

First, adjust your attitude to failure. Every failure is nothing more than an opportunity to do a better job next time. Or as I like to put it: there is no such thing as failure—only forced growth.

Second, learn all that you can from every apparent failure. I say *apparent* because until you come to the end of your life, you will never know whether the bad thing that happened to you was really a curse or blessing in disguise.

Third, learn to forget your failures. There is no greater handicap in life than a perfect memory—a memory that hoards failures. These

> If you make room for failure, you can overcome it.

memories rob you of confidence and get in the way of trying new things.

Fourth, learn to revise, or even create, new expectations. The biggest mistake anyone can make here is to hold on to out-of-date expectations. Yes, set goals, but they are there only to give you some direction. When circumstances warrant it, change them.

Fifth, always rejoice in your successes. Celebrate them. Then remind yourself of how your failures contributed to your successes, and thus reinforce a positive attitude to your disappointment and apparent failures. If you can do this, you are a winner all the way. And the joy it will bring will overshadow all the pain you picked up on the way.

[a final word]

We are a pleasure-seeking society. We spend our energy seeking pleasure and avoiding pain. We hope by doing this we will feel happy. But deep, abiding, and authentic happiness eludes many people.

Whereas anhedonia was once considered to be the cardinal symptom of serious emotional disorders, it is now pervasively present in our day. Our children and grandchildren are particularly vulnerable, given the high level of stimulation and excitement they are exposed to.

There was a time when the pursuit of pleasure was labeled as *hedonistic* by philosophers and considered to be unhealthy by many psychologists. But modern brain science, especially brain imaging techniques, has restored pleasure's importance. But in this book, I have taken our newfound respect for pleasure a step further and proposed that much of life's enjoyments, including the elusive happiness, is directly linked to the brain's pleasure system. If you mess up your pleasure system, say by an addiction or other form of overstimulation, you also destroy your ability to appreciate the things in life that help you to become enduringly happy.

In some small way, I trust that I have helped you come to a new appreciation of your brain's pleasure system. You need to nurture it by seeking the right sort of pleasure and teaching your children how to do the same. Their happiness, as well as the happiness of their children depends on it.

I also trust that I have helped Christian readers see how their faith and its benefits can contribute to a more abundant life. Much of the help that I have shared has strong theological roots for me. Also, I find that the positive psychology movement, which has a strong focus on building authentic happiness in people's lives as a buffer against mental illness, is very integrative with my faith.

Whether pleasure, as we are coming to understand it scientifically, will aid in integrating mind and spirit remains to be seen. All I know is that as I have begun to respect my pleasure system and cooperate with the brain mechanisms that foster happiness, I have also begun to experience a much deeper and more fulfilling spiritual life. My hope is that you will be able to do the same.

[recovering your pleasure]

DISCUSSION QUESTIONS FOR PERSONAL OR GROUP STUDY

Chapter 1: Where Has All Our Pleasure Gone?
1. What does anhedonia feel like to you?
2. What areas of your life, and the lives of your loved ones, are most affected by anhedonia?
3. Can you identify any activity in your life that may be contributing to your loss of ability to experience pleasure?

Chapter 2: The Many Pathways to Pleasure
1. There are several causes of modern anhedonia, each using its unique pathway to the pleasure center in the brain. What do they all have in common? Which of these causes or pathways puts you at risk for losing all your pleasure ability?
2. Feelings of apathy will overcome all of us at some time or other. This is normal and to be expected. But when does a state of apathy become unhealthy?
3. After you have taken the test for anhedonia in this chapter, reflect back on your life and try to identify a time when your pleasure system was healthier.

Chapter 3: Pleasure or Happiness?

1. How do pleasure and happiness differ in your experience?

2. What in your present life is robbing you of happiness? What from your past life may be robbing you of pleasure?

3. The idea that happiness has an immovable set point is quite popular even though it is a myth. True, many people don't seem able to improve their happiness, but what happiness boosters should you consider exploring?

Chapter 4: Stress and Anhedonia

1. In what ways does your lifestyle contribute to the difficulties you are having in getting pleasure out of the simple things of life?

2. Can you identify activities in your life that are stimulating to the point of recruiting high levels of adrenaline? Can you reduce these activities?

3. How much has your pleasure system been affected by the advent of the Internet? What is it about the Internet that has robbed you of deep contentment? Are there any changes you need to make in your life in order to lower your stress level?

Chapter 5: Saving Our Children from Anhedonia

1. Without a doubt, childhood today is very threatening to both happiness and the brain's pleasure system. What areas in a child's life should parents be particularly wary of?

2. Teenage multitasking is being both applauded (by industry and business) and condemned (by brain researchers). How does excessive multitasking impact the learning ability, the social development, and anhedonia in a developing child?

3. Identify three do's and three don'ts that parents should consider in guiding their children's multitasking activities.

Chapter 6: When Pleasure Becomes a Hidden Addiction

1. How do hidden addictions differ from substance addictions? Can some hidden addictions be as hazardous as substance addictions?
2. Why are all addictions capable of robbing us of pleasure in the little things of life? Try and identify at least three hidden addictions in your life.
3. Obsessions with work and the Internet are now considered to be the most pervasive hidden addictions that can create anhedonia. To what extent are you vulnerable in both these areas?

Chapter 7: Sexual Anhedonia

1. Sexual anhedonia and low sexual drive are often indistinguishable. What are the important symptoms that can tell the one from the other?
2. What are the more common causes of sexual anhedonia, as opposed to low sexual drive—in men versus women?
3. What are some of the ways that men can repair and build a healthier sexual pleasure response? What challenges do women face in the area of sexual anhedonia?

Chapter 8: Step 1—Seek the Right Form of Pleasure

1. How do type A pleasures differ from type B pleasures? How can the one help to repair the damage done by the other?
2. Try to identify several of your vulnerable pleasure points—where you look for pleasure in the wrong places.

3. Of the several pleasure boosters identified in this chapter, which is most important for your life? In what ways can you enhance the pleasure boosters you have been neglecting?

Chapter 9: Step 2—Recapture the Joy of Little Things

1. What are the *best pleasures of all* in your life?
2. Discovering your past is a very helpful tool for enhancing present day happiness. Recall some of the happiest moments of your childhood and then write a brief story or poem to capture these moments so you can continue to remind yourself of them.
3. What games did you play as a child that were pleasurable? When you have an opportunity, teach your children (or someone else's children) some of these games and take some time to play them together.

Chapter 10: Step 3—Control Your Adrenaline

1. Since the brain cannot tolerate constant pleasure or stimulation, it is important that the pleasure system have time for recovery. What three critical areas of your life can provide this rest time for the brain's pleasure center?
2. Why is it that you have difficulty slowing down? What new habits can you develop that can help you to take it easy?
3. Look at the list of baby steps for lowering your stress, and reorder them in their level of importance for your life. Use this list as your prescription for stress control.

Chapter 11: Step 4—Use Humor to Enhance Your Happiness

1. Why is laughter so beneficial to the human body?

2. In what areas do you need to focus on building your laughter quotient?

3. Take a moment and try to recall at least three incidents from the last week that were funny enough to make you laugh.

Chapter 12: Step 5—Develop Appreciation and Gratitude

1. Examine again the differences between appreciation and gratitude, and recall an example of each out of your recent life.

2. In what ways can you strengthen your appreciation ability?

3. What are the main ingredients in the Glad Game, the Gratitude Game, and the "I Wish You Enough" Game?

Chapter 13: Step 6—Master Relaxation and Meditation

1. What scientific evidence is there for the value of relaxation to both the body and mind?

2. How does meditation work?

3. What different forms of mediation do you find appealing?

Chapter 14: Step 7—Make Space for the Things That Matter

1. What things in life really matter to you? Make a list and display it where you can see it often.

2. What bad things tend to get in the way of the things that matter to you, and what can you do to remove them?

3. If you cannot remove the bad things that cause you pain, what redeeming features can help you tolerate or bypass their negative consequences?

[appendix a]

HOW TO ORDER DR. HART'S
RELAXATION TRAINING CD

The *Relaxation and Christian Meditation* CD is designed to do four things:

1. It will help you develop the ability to rapidly produce a deep state of muscle relaxation, called the *relaxation response*. This response minimizes your body's arousal systems, including your adrenaline, cortisol, and other *sad messengers* and maximizes your *happy messengers*.

2. It will teach you how to warm your hands as a way of switching off your fight-or-flight response. The *cold hands* phenomenon is particularly prevalent in those who easily trigger their adrenaline response or who are under high stress.

3. It will teach you how to take control of your thoughts and redirect them, in times of worry or high anxiety, into more constructive channels. Included in this section will be training in how to cut off your worrying.

4. It will provide you with a way you can enhance your sensory awareness of what is going on around you and participate in Christian-based meditation exercises.

APPENDIX A

You can order this audio CD direct from Dr. Hart for a cost of $10, including postage. Put your name and address on a three-by-five inch piece of paper (serves as an address label) and send it along with your check to:

Dr. Archibald Hart
1042 Cyrus Lane
Arcadia, CA 91006

[appendix b]

ADDITIONAL RESOURCES

Books

Hart, Archibald D., *The Sexual Man*. Dallas: Word, 1994.

————, *The Hidden Link between Adrenaline and Stress*. Nashville: W Publishing Group, 1995.

————, *Unmasking Male Depression*. Nashville: W Publishing Group, 2001.

Hart, Archibald D. and Weber, Catherine Hart. *Unveiling Depression in Women: A Practical Guide to Understanding and Overcoming Depression*. Grand Rapids: Revell, 2002.

————, *Stressed or Depressed: A Practical and Inspirational Guide for Parents of Hurting Teens*. Nashville: Integrity, 2005.

Peterson, Christopher, and Martin Seligman, *Character Strengths and Virtues*. New York: Oxford University Press, 2004.

Seligman Martin, *Learned Optimism*. New York: Knopf, 1990.

————, *Authentic Happiness*. New York: Free Press, 2004.

Snyder, C. R. and Sharon Lopez, *Positive Psychology: The Scientific and Practical Explorations of Human Strengths*. Thousand Oaks, CA: Sage Publications, 2007.

Internet Resources

A. Anhedonia

1. Information about anhedonia:

     www.en.wikipedia.org/wiki/Anhedonia

     www.netdoctor.co.uk/special_reports/depression/

     anhedonia.htm

     www.unlockyourlife.com/unlock/htm/ul2.html

     www.mindandmuscle.net/forum/

     index.php?showtopic=22197&hl=glutamate

2. Article about pleasure:

     www.plato.stanford.edu/entries/pleasure/notes.html

3. Pleasure systems in the brain:

     www.wings.buffalo.edu/aru/ARUreport01.htm

4. Depression and sadness:

     www.aafp.org/afp/990901ap/820.html

     www.depression.about.com/cs/amidepressed/a/sadness.htm

     www.mcmanweb.com

5. Coping with the loss of pleasure:

     www.thehealthcenter.info/emotions/loss-of-pleasure/

     coping.htm

B: Christian Meditation

1. God, pleasure, and other sources of joy:

     www.miketaylor.org.uk/xian/pleasure.html

     www.desiringgod/.org

C. Happiness and Pleasure

    1. Articles relating to happiness and pleasure:

        www.pages.slu.edu/faculty/haybrond/Happiness%20and
           %20Pleasure.pdf

        www.nupathz.com/wow/Other/Happiness_Versus_
           Pleasure.htm

        www.authentichappiness.org

    2. How can you find happiness?

        www.reflectivehappiness.com/AboutUs/LTimes

D. Healthy Eating

    1. Excellent healthy eating resources for children:

        www.kidsnutrition.org/consumer/nyc/healthyeating.htm

    2. Healthy eating resources for weight loss:

        www.healthyeating.net/he_4-05.htm

    3. Smart nutrition guidelines:

        www.nutrition.gov

E. Positive Psychology

        www.reflectivehappiness.com

[notes]

Chapter 1: Where Has All Our Pleasure Gone?

1. "No Pleasure, No Reward—Plenty of Depression," McMan's Depression and Bipolar Web, John McManamy, www.mcmanweb.com/no_pleasure.htm.

Chapter 2: The Many Pathways to Pleasure

1. "When Your Brain Goes Crash—Depression," McMan's Depression and Bipolar Web, John McManamy, www.mcmanweb.com/depression.htm.

Chapter 3: Pleasure or Happiness?

1. "The Biology of Joy," *Time* vol. 165, no.3, 17 January 2005.
2. Zak Stambor, "A Key to Happiness," *Monitor on Psychology* (American Psychological Association), October 2006, 34.
3. Wilfred McClay, "A Short History of Happiness," *Implications*, 12 December 2006, www.ttf.org/index/journal/detail/short-history-of-happiness.
4. Archibald D. Hart, *15 Principles for Achieving Happiness* (Dallas: Word Books, 1988).
5. Ibid.
6. "Money Can't Buy Happiness," BBC News, 2 February 2001, www.news.bbc.co.uk/1/hi/health/1162153.stm.

Chapter 4: Stress and Anhedonia

1. J. L. Moreau, "Simulation of a Core Symptom of Human Depression in Rats," *Current Topics in Pharmacology*, 4:37–50.
2. "Sense-sational: Celebrate and Sharpen All Your Senses," CNN.com Health Report, 22 January 2007, www.cnn.com/2007/HEALTH/ 01/22/healthmag.senses/index.html.
3. Archibald D. Hart, *The Hidden Link Between Adrenaline and Stress* (Dallas: W Publishing Group, 1995).

Chapter 5: Saving Our Children from Anhedonia

1. Claudia Wallis, "Are Kids Too Wired for Their Own Good?" *Time*, 27 March 2006, 23.
2. Madeline Levine, *The Price of Privilege* (New York: HarperCollins, 2006), 3.
3. "But I Want It Now!!!" House of Joy, 23 Feb. 2005, www.houseofjoy.blogspot.com/2005_02_01_archive.html.
4. Lindsey Tanner, "Resorting to Self-Injury: Students Inflicting Wounds to Express Angst," *Pasadena Star News*, 6 June 2006.
5. Jim Dryden, "Depression in Preschoolers," Washington University in St. Louis News & Information, http://mednews.wustl.edu/tips/ page/normal/4172.html.
6. Archibald Hart and Catherine Weber, *Stressed or Depressed* (Nashville: Integrity, 2005).
7. "The Importance of Play in Promoting Healthy Child Development and Maintaining Strong Parent-Child Bonds," American Academy of Pediatrics, www.aap.org/pressroom/playFINAL.pdf.

Chapter 6: When Pleasure Becomes a Hidden Addiction

1. See various studies cited at www.worklifebalance.org.
2. Associated Press, "Americans Addicted to High-Tech Gadgets," 21 December 2005, www.msnbc.msn.com/id/10558581.
3. William Glasser, *Positive Addiction* (San Francisco: Harper and Row, 1976).
4. Gerald May, *Addiction and Grace* (New York: Harper Collins, 1988).

Chapter 7: Sexual Anhedonia

1. Robert T. Michael et. al., *Sex in America: A Definitive Survey* (New York: Warner, 1995).
2. "Loving With All Your . . . Brain," CNN.com Health Report, 14 February 2007, www.cnn.com/2007/HEALTH/02/14/ love.science/index.html.
3. Archibald D. Hart, *The Sexual Man* (Dallas: Word Books, 1994), 34.

Chapter 8: Step 1—Seek the Right Form of Pleasure

1. Sadie F. Dingfelder, "Why We Sleep," *Monitor on Psychology*, January 2006, 50–58.
2. "Wake Up America—A National Sleep Alert," *Report of the National Commission on Sleep Disorders Research*, United States Department of Health and Human Services, 1995.
3. Various surveys available at www.chpa-info.org/ChpaPortal/ International.
4. "Why is me time such a big deal?" CNN.com Health Report, 15 September 2006, www.cnn.com/2006/HEALTH/09/15/ me.time.health/index/html.

Chapter 9: Step 2—Recapture the Joy of Little Things

1. "We Have This Moment Today," lyrics by Gloria Gaither, music by William J. Gaither, © 1975 William J. Gaither.
2. Archibald D. Hart, *The Hidden Link Between Adrenaline and Stress* (Dallas: W Publishing Group, 1995).

Chapter 11: Step 4—Use Humor to Enhance Your Happiness

1. Examples of humor found on www.speicher.com/humor2a.htm.

Chapter 12: Step 5—Develop Appreciation and Gratitude

1. Martin Seligman, "Gratitude," *Review of General Psychology*, vol. 9, no. 2, 111–31.

Chapter 13: Step 6—Master Relaxation and Meditation

1. Calvin Woodward, "AP Poll Finds Americans in a Hurry," *Pasadena Star News*, Associated Press report, 29 May 2006, A9.
2. Edmund Jacobson, MD, *You Must Relax*, 4th ed. (New York: McGraw-Hill, 1962).
13. Charles H. Spurgeon, "Meditation," www.the-highway.com/meditation_Spurgeon.html.

Chapter 14: Step 7—Make Space for the Things That Matter

1. Lewis B. Smedes, *My God and I: A Spiritual Memoir* (Grand Rapids: Eerdmans, 2003), 175.
2. Archibald Hart and Sharon Hart Morris, *Safe Haven Marriage* (Nashville: W Publishing Group, 2003).
3. Sonja Steptoe, "Ready, Set, Relax!" *Time*, 22 October 2003.
4. "First study to watch brain patterns when forgiving," www.eurekalert.org/pub_releases/2003-10/cff-fst100803.php.
5. Archibald D. Hart, *15 Principles for Achieving Happiness* (Dallas: Word Books, 1988).
6. Archibald D. Hart, *Habits of the Mind* (Dallas: W Publishing Group, 1996).